SURVEY AND REPAIR OF TRADITIONAL BUILDINGS

A Sustainable Approach

SURVEY AND
REPAIR OF
TRADITIONAL BUILDINGS
A Sustainable Approach

Richard Oxley

DONHEAD

Published in the United Kingdom in 2003 by Donhead Publishing.

Donhead Publishing
Lower Coombe
Donhead St Mary
Shaftesbury
Dorset SP7 9LY
Tel: +44 (0)1747 828422
www.donhead.com

ISBN 1 873394 50 0

Printed in Great Britain by Bath Press

British Library Cataloguing in Publication Data

Oxley, Richard
Survey and Repair of Traditional Buildings : a sustainable approach
1.Building inspection – Great Britain 2.Surveying – Great Britain
3.Historic buildings – conservation and restoration – Great Britain
I.Title
690.2'0941

ISBN 1873394500
Library of Congress Cataloguing in Publication Data
A catalog record for this book has been requested

This book has been printed from paper produced from sustainable resources

For Billy

CONTENTS

ACKNOWLEDGEMENTS

This book reflects my development as a surveyor and my interest and passion for building conservation. This journey would not have possible without the positive guidance and inspiration of the many people I have encountered. This is an opportunity to say a special thank you to some of those people who have helped me along the way.

Kane Yeardley, Richard Robinson, Steve Potter, Hugh Pavitt, Nicola Sterry, Ian Pritchett, Marion Brinton, Neil May, Tracey Hartley, Russ Craig, Mike Dunn, David Arnold, and Peter Warm.

All those who have produced some of the fine examples of workmanship illustrated in this book, in particular: Paul Turnham, Dan Barton, John Mitchell, John Lloyd and their colleagues.

The owners and those responsible for the care of the buildings I have had the privilege to work with.

The course tutors of the RICS Diploma in Building Conservation at the College of Estate Management, Reading.

The Society for the Protection of Ancient Buildings.

Everyone who has helped in producing this book, with a special mention for:

John Gleeson for asking me to write a book in the first place.

Phillip Hartley and Mary Craig for their constructive input and guidance.

Robin Dukes for helping with the test panels.

Everyone at Donhead; Jill Pearce for all her patience and prompting, Dorothy Newberry for pulling it all together and Sarah Sutton for her input to the final draft.

A special mention for Alan Gardner for his enthusiasm and friendship.

To Sally and Billy for maintaining their unstinting support and love.

The past is part of my future
The present is well out of hand

Heart and soul
Joy Division

PREFACE

The survey is the starting point for advice and recommendations in the care and repair of buildings. When surveying or repairing a traditional building the practitioner therefore needs to adopt an approach that reflects the manner of its construction and intended performance. All too often, decisions are made that are based upon an approach that is more relevant to modern buildings.

Approximately a quarter of all buildings in the UK are of traditional construction, which in simplistic terms means that they are constructed with solid rather than cavity walls. This elementary difference between traditional and modern buildings is not always taken into account during the survey or when recommendations for repairs are made. As a result, traditional buildings are frequently treated in the same way as those of modern construction. This is a recipe for disaster, as it invariably leads to inappropriate advice or recommendations that are detrimental to the condition of many traditional buildings.

The book reflects my concerns regarding the existing and future condition of a significant percentage of the building stock. It sets out an approach to the survey and repair of traditional buildings that will help practitioners and their clients prevent well-intentioned recommendations and repairs from damaging the very buildings they are setting out to look after. This approach is needed to counteract existing survey and repair practices that are contributing to the unnecessary loss and accelerated deterioration of what is a valuable and irreplaceable resource. It is an approach that will allow the practitioner to put their skills into practice in a way that is appropriate to traditional buildings, and will assist in improving the management of a vulnerable finite resource so that sustainable goals can be met.

Current practices are not sustainable, as they do not meet the needs of the present and will compromise the ability of future generations to meet their own requirements. The reasons for this situation are complex and will be difficult to address; nevertheless, the severity of the consequences means that doing nothing is not an option. This generation must try to make a difference. This book illustrates how an understanding of a building's performance can make a positive contribution to the future sustainability of a significant percentage of the existing building stock.

The survey is a primary starting point for properly identifying the condition of a building and its problems. The property professional has a crucial and positive role to play in improving the way buildings are surveyed and cared for so that we can realise a well-maintained and sustainable building stock. At present, surveys are often inadequate and standards have to be raised. To achieve this will require examination of existing practices across the building industry, for weaknesses to be identified, and appropriate changes made. This is a challenge for all property professionals, but is one that we cannot avoid if we are to act in a responsible and accountable way that will benefit this and future generations.

The lessons learnt in the development of building conservation, particularly over the last twenty years or so, provide a sound basis from which to devise an approach that is appropriate to the survey and repair of traditional buildings. But for such an approach to become commonplace, and therefore to have a real influence, a new direction is required – one that moves away from assessments made solely according to architectural and historical importance, to one that is as inclusive as possible, and applicable to as many buildings as possible. Only then will any real progress be made.

While the architectural or historical interest of buildings is of vital importance and must be treated with respect, we have to assess the condition and performance of all traditional buildings in the same manner. To advocate an approach to the survey, repair and maintenance of buildings that is based purely on the grounds of whether a building is of architectural or historic interest excludes a significant number of buildings that have the same needs and requirements, and which are an important and valuable resource. For example, in order to properly maintain a traditional building, a solid wall needs to perform as intended, allowing moisture to readily evaporate, irrespective of whether it is listed or not. This fundamental principle must be taken into account when carrying out a survey or instigating repairs. If it is not, that is when problems can start.

The retention and appropriate repair and maintenance of traditional buildings can be justified on environmental grounds. At the forefront of all our decisions should be the need to make a positive contribution to protect and enhance the environment, and to halt further degradation. A change in approach is needed to ensure that existing resources are properly managed. This can only be achieved by developing sustainable practices that are based on a holistic approach.

The fundamental principles needed to adopt such an approach are set out in the following chapters, and are intended to provide a basis from which informed and reasoned decisions can be made – to assist practitioners in the survey process when recommending or specifying repairs, and in order to avoid repeating the mistakes made by previous generations. Rather than try to provide prescriptive solutions, which is not possible when working with older buildings, I have outlined an approach that will enable the practitioner to appreciate what to expect and what to look for; and to provide some guidance on how to put a sustainable, green, approach to the repair and survey of traditional buildings into practice.

With this in mind I have collated the factors to be taken into account when surveying and repairing traditional buildings, while deliberately avoiding the repetition of general principles of surveying which are amply covered in other publications. There is an emphasis on the approach required to achieve sustainable solutions, rather than the provision of highly detailed guidance, as the diversity of the existing building stock would make this a daunting task. I have relied on information that I find invaluable in my day-to-day work and use case studies to illustrate the problems that can be encountered, and show how they may be overcome.

I have written this book with the property professional in mind, but not to the exclusion of the owner or non-professional who has an interest in the appropriate repair and maintenance of traditional buildings. For the purpose of this book the property professional, or practitioner, is anyone who encounters traditional buildings in their day-to-day work, from architects, surveyors, loss adjustors, structural and civil engineers, service engineers and conservation officers and their professional institutions, to those who carry out the work (such as builders, developers and damp and timber contractors), those who supply materials, and those who have a control and influence on how buildings are surveyed and repaired (banks and building societies, insurers and the legal professions).

My hope is that this book will stimulate interest and debate and ultimately, provoke positive action, so that we improve our understanding, and start to take responsibility for the environmental impact of our decisions. By doing this we can and will make a difference.

Richard Oxley
January 2003

INTRODUCTION

1

WHAT IS A TRADITIONAL BUILDING?

This book assesses and categorises buildings according to the manner of their construction and intended performance but does not rely solely on whether a building is formally recognised and protected as being of architectural or historic interest. It defines a building of traditional construction as one that is of a solid wall construction built with porous fabric that both absorbs and readily allows the evaporation of moisture.

For the purpose of this book a traditional building is a 'breathing' building; this can be a church, a house, a commercial or industrial building or even a ruin. This is in contrast with most modern buildings that are constructed in impervious materials designed to exclude moisture and that rely upon physical barriers such as damp proof courses, membranes and cavity walls. These fundamental differences are expanded upon in Chapter 5.

Figures 1.1a, 1.1b, 1.1c and 1.1d Traditionally constructed buildings are diverse in their size, shape and form as well as the materials of construction. The one thing that the buildings illustrated have in common is that they are of solid wall construction and rely on the ability of moisture to evaporate from the fabric.

Figure 1.1a

Figure 1.1b

Figure 1.1c

Figure 1.1d

THE TYPES OF SURVEY

Every day the existing building stock is exposed to many different types of inspection and survey and clear differentiation needs to be made between traditional and modern buildings in order to encourage better understanding of the true condition of the buildings, thereby reducing the occurrence of surveys that cause damaging work.

Buildings of all types can be subject to one of more or the following:

- *Valuations*
  Mortgage valuations
  Risk assessments – a basic evaluation made by mortgage lenders
  Commercial valuations
  Portfolio assessments
- *Surveys*
  Pre-purchase surveys
  Vendors surveys (Home Condition Report)
  RICS Homebuyer Survey and Valuation Report
  Building Surveys and Condition Surveys
  Structural Survey/Assessments
- *Buildings in continued ownership*
  Periodic condition inspection reports (e.g. Quinquennial
    InspectionReports, such as those carried out by The National
    Trust and the Church of England)
- *Defect analysis investigations*
- *Damp and timber surveys*
- *Investigations into structural movement*

- *Schedule of dilapidations*
- *Feasibility studies*
- *Specifications for repair*
- *Designs for alteration*
- *Insurance claims – including the specification of repair for damage suffered*
- *Energy assessments and ratings*
- *Grant aid applications*

Each type of survey has the potential for inappropriate recommendations to be made and for instigating unsympathetic and damaging repair. The many types and forms of survey also illustrate the considerable cumulative influence that it can have on the condition of traditional buildings, so a practitioner carrying out any of the types of survey itemised above on a traditional building needs to be aware of the potentially detrimental impact inappropriate advice can have. This book highlights the factors that need to be taken into account when carrying out a survey or instigating repair works to traditional buildings.

PROFESSIONAL RESPONSIBILITY

As can be seen, the role of the property professional is deeply entwined with the current and future condition of the existing building stock. This is a responsibility that cannot be taken lightly. Property professionals, by virtue of their specialist knowledge, are expected to act in the best interests of the buildings they inspect and survey. This reasonable assumption is usually only challenged when they make mistakes; when they act negligently in the advice or the recommendations they make.

To achieve an understanding of the practices involved in the survey process we need to assess the 'democratic intellect' or accountability, of property professionals; the manner in which many inspect and survey the existing building stock, in particular those buildings of a traditional construction.

'Democratic intellect' – the notion that while knowledge inevitably creates specialists, the value of that specialism will be fully disclosed only when its inevitable blind spots are put to the test in real-life service and accountability to the community.[1]

When current practices are put under scrutiny the way that property professionals approach the survey of the existing building stock and their real-life service and accountability to the community can be found wanting. If property professionals wish their specialism to be properly valued and respected, existing practices have to change.

This book explains and illustrates the reasons for this need for change and provides an approach that can improve the ways in which traditional buildings are surveyed and repaired. This will simultaneously achieve cultural, social, economic and environmental benefits and is therefore, by definition, a sustainable approach.

THE INFLUENCE OF THE SURVEY

The results of a survey will in many cases influence the extent and manner in which a building is altered, repaired and maintained, as well as how resources are used and consumed in the process. It is the critical stage at which the way a building is managed and its future well-being are decided. A survey provides a direct link between how we manage not only the building but also the demands we make on the earth's resources.

Throughout this book, case studies are provided that illustrate how the survey can have a negative influence on the condition of the existing building stock; principally where there has been a lack of appreciation of the differences between older, traditional, and modern buildings.

Practitioners make recommendations for repair based upon their personal experience and knowledge, and will, by virtue of their education and training, be most familiar with modern conventional structures and the principles of repair and maintenance appropriate to modern buildings. On this basis, the practitioner is more likely to fail to recognise that many commonly used modern materials and methods are incompatible with the performance of traditional buildings. Any survey or recommendations for repair based upon such limited awareness will inevitably lead to problems of misdiagnosis.

The importance and influence of the survey must not be underestimated. It is the natural point at which all interested parties will focus on and discuss the needs of the building, and is therefore the ideal place to start to try and reverse the adverse effects of existing practices, and where an approach based upon an appreciation and understanding of the buildings being inspected can be put into practice.

WHAT IS THE EXTENT OF THE PROBLEM?

The true condition of the existing building stock is unknown, but there appears to be a common assumption that it is in a generally sound and serviceable condition. This assumption is based largely upon knowledge of the principles of repair and maintenance appropriate to modern buildings, so where this philosophy is likely to have been applied, the condition of the building stock needs to be reassessed, as illustrated in the following two case studies:

Case Study 1.1 **A negligent survey?**

In this case a surveyor carried out a pre-purchase survey on a Grade II listed timber-framed building. After occupying the building the new owner became concerned about the condition of the timber frame to the exposed gable of the building, as decay was identified by a decorator. As a result, a further report was provided by a different surveyor and an estimate of the cost of repairing the gable was produced by a specialist builder. These revealed the extent of decay and put the cost of repair at much more than the sum specified in the original survey. Legal proceedings were instigated and the case went to court.

The judge found that the condition of the gable wall at the date of the original pre-purchase survey was as follows:

1. There was deep-seated rot in many timbers.
2. There was extensive, poor quality, cement patching, in particular over many of the joints.
3. The cement patch repairs were loose in many places, especially at the joints.

The judge said, 'The defendant did fail to exercise reasonable skill and care in reporting to and advising the plaintiff on the results of his inspection', for the following reasons:

The matters (1) to (3) above would have led a competent building surveyor exercising reasonable skill and care to the conclusion that there was at the very least a real risk of widespread wet rot affecting the structural integrity of the wall in a serious way and would have led to him advising that further inspection needed to be carried out. If such further inspection had been advised and carried out, it would undoubtedly have revealed the true and dangerous state of the wall.

The report and, in particular, its conclusion did not, in my judgment, accurately reflect the true and dangerous state of the wall. It did not convey the concern about the joints or timber frame itself, nor did the report follow the 'trail of suspicion'.[2]

The first survey did not warn the purchaser of potential problems as the readily available warning signs were not heeded. The fundamental difference between traditional and modern buildings was not appreciated, understood or conveyed. Consequently a building was bought that was not in as good condition as the purchaser had been lead to believe, in this case resulting in legal action against the surveyor.

Figure 1.2a A detail of the part of the gable before dismantling works had commenced. Note the cement patch repairs, and use of impervious paint to decorate the timber frame and infill panels. *Courtesy of IJP Building Conservation*

Figure 1.2b A detail of the same part of the gable after removal of the infill panels. Note the severe decay to the structural joints of the timbers that were concealed by the cement patch repairs. The adverse impact of impervious materials is appreciated when they are removed. *Courtesy of IJP Building Conservation*

Case Study 1.2 Haddenham Methodist Church

Figure 1.3 Grade II listed church constructed in wychert, concealed by render.

This case study concerns the collapse of the south-west wychert wall of a Grade II listed church located in a conservation area. Wychert or witchert, meaning 'white mud', is the term applied to earth walling in Buckinghamshire, found in particular around the village of Haddenham.

The building was constructed in 1822 as a Wesleyan Chapel. During building works to remove damaged internal plaster the south-west wall collapsed, luckily no one was injured. These works were in effect treating the symptoms of a more serious problem, as illustrated in the collapse of the wall. The practitioner in this case did not anticipate the poor condition of the wall when instigating repairs, although there were sufficient warning signs. The principal reasons for the collapse included:

1. The flanks walls were large and had very little lateral restraint or support.
2. The slender thickness-to-height ratio of the wall made it particularly sensitive to any changes.
3. The wall in question was south-west facing and therefore exposed to the prevailing weather.
4. The introduction of impervious renders, mortars, plasters and paints resulted in a change from the intended traditional breathing performance. The attempts to exclude the weather failed as the hard and rigid materials cracked, allowing water to

enter the fabric. The impervious nature of the renders and paints resulted in moisture and salts becoming entrapped and displaced within the walls.
5. The application of the cement-based rendering created poor weathering detailing to the verges and plinths.
6. Previous flood irrigation treatment against dry rot had introduced significant levels of water and chemicals into the structure (figure 1.6). This remedial treatment will have significantly weakened the structural stability of the wall and the chemicals used probably introduced salts into the walls. The treatment was carried out to the base of the walls, which is a vulnerable part of an earth wall. The water and salts became entrapped by the cement renders and plasters.
7. The salts in the wall, originating from ground salts in the earth used to construct the walls, as well as from the chemical treatment, will have been mobilised by the presence of excess water. The crystallisation of salts will have weakened the condition of the wall and caused the separation of the cement plaster from the wall (figure 1.4 shows the wall immediately prior to collapse).
8. The intermittent use and heating of the building together with inadequate ventilation will have provided the conditions for both surface and interstitial condensation to take place.
9. Extreme weather conditions suffered in recent years will have exacerbated and accelerated the structural weakening of the wall.
10. Physical intervention to remove plasters will have disturbed the sensitive state of equilibrium of the wall.

As can be seen, a number of factors contributed to the collapse of the south-west wall. The practitioner who initiated the works did not take these into consideration, and as a result was not put on notice of the extent of the potential problems and associated dangers at the building. Consequently, works were instigated that treated the symptoms of failure – the repair of the salt-damaged internal plasters (figure 1.4). These disturbed the sensitive structural equilibrium and resulted in the collapse of the wall.

Investigations revealed that the dry rot irrigation treatment introduced into the earth walls had used tributyl tin oxide (TBTO) and lindane. These chemicals are no longer in common use as they are recognised as having an unacceptable impact in environmental terms and are a risk to humans who come into contact with them, with the dust from the collapse being a particular health risk.[3,4] The potential health hazards of the chemicals remain many years after treatment, offering stark warning of the need to be accountable to future generations for the materials we use.

The irrigation treatment for dry rot is acknowledged as being of limited use as it is a method that requires large volumes of fluid. The extensive use of fluids inhibits the drying out of the walls thereby increasing the risk of dry rot spreading to adjacent areas rather than containing the fungal decay as intended. Irrigation also carries the risk of salt efflorescence that can cause damage to decorations.[5]

In this case, the true condition of the building had not been appreciated. This resulted in a classic case of treating the symptoms rather than the causes of the problems. The dry rot treatment contributed to the structural damage suffered by the earth wall and probably caused more harm than any outbreak of dry rot could have.

Acting without appreciating the likely condition of the building and the potential problems hastened the structural failure of the wall.

Figure 1.4 (above left) The damaged internal plaster before removal.

Figure 1.5 (above right) The collapse of the south-west wall.

Figure 1.6 (left) Holes in the wychert wall, the result of fluid irrigation treatment against dry rot.

Do these two case studies provide an indication as to the true condition of many traditional buildings? The answer is we do not know; but I am sure that if we look more closely, on an informed basis, we will find that the condition of a significant percentage of the existing building stock needs to be drastically re-evaluated. The serviceability and longevity of many buildings will be called into question if their structural condition is more closely examined and the extent and rates of decay noted. The principal reason for this is that it is unfortunately very rare to encounter older buildings that have escaped the use of modern materials and methods of repair. Case Studies 1.1 and 1.2 reflect the type of problems that can be commonly encountered when surveying traditional buildings, and indicate the potential enormity of the task ahead.

The case studies also illustrate that practitioners who do not recognise where repairs are inappropriate and damaging to the building fabric cannot be relied upon to identify that a problem exists in the first place, nor to make recommendations to address the causes. In these circumstances recommendations will inevitably be made that treat the symptoms only, thus allowing the cause of the problem to continue until serious damage is suffered. Failure to identify and distinguish between old and new construction methods will eventually exacerbate the problems. Recommendations for repair that rely solely on modern materials actually cause physical damage; accelerate rates of decay; and lead to the loss of irreplaceable fabric.

This is not just a peripheral or isolated problem. Approximately a quarter of all dwellings in the UK were constructed before 1918, the vast majority of these being of a traditional construction.[6] This estimate does not include the many industrial, commercial and other building types. Between the First and Second World Wars many buildings were still being constructed with solid walls and it was only after the Second World War that traditional construction effectively ceased in the UK. As can be seen, traditional buildings comprise a significant percentage of the built environment and therefore need to be given the due consideration that their numbers deserve.

It is also important to appreciate that these buildings will be subjected to external pressures that will often result in damaging work. For example, buildings will inevitably be exposed to varying degrees of maintenance, repair and alteration when they are bought and sold. Buildings are at their most vulnerable during a change in ownership, but, importantly, this is also the time when the survey can have a positive influence.

To put the extent of the problem into perspective, and in a way that we can relate to, simply take a walk around any city, town or village. This will reveal that it is extremely difficult to identify a single building that retains its traditional finishes, or to find a building that has not been repaired or maintained with inappropriate and incompatible materials, such as modern paints and cement renders and pointing. It is the exception rather than the rule to find a building that has escaped intervention with modern materials and continues to be repaired and maintained using traditional materials and methods consistent and compatible with the intended performance.

As a result, the actual condition and future repairing liabilities of the building stock needs to be reassessed, a significant amount of work is required to remove, halt or at least slow down the rates of decay, to rectify the damage suffered and to arrive at a position where appropriate routine repair and maintenance can be implemented.

To allow the erosion of fabric that still has a useful life to continue does not make practical, cultural, social, economic or environmental sense. Traditional buildings have an important role to play as they can inform this and future generations of the development of cultures, enabling them to learn from both their successes and failures. They illustrate the importance and value of longevity and how this can be achieved with minimal cost to the environment. If we want a sustainable future, to pass on something worthwhile to our decedents, we have to work with what we have and not against it.

> There should be a general presumption in favour of preservation: no
> element of the built heritage should be lost without adequate and careful
> consideration of its significance and of all the means available to
> conserve it.[7]

THE ROLE OF THE PROPERTY PROFESSIONAL

> ... we cannot rely on legislation to determine behaviour. It is still necessary
> to change attitudes and this must be done through education of professionals
> and others in the construction industry in particular about the implications
> of specification decisions on the environment.[8]

The property professional plays the principal role in the survey of buildings, and will have inevitably contributed to the legacy of decay that this generation has inherited. However, property professionals will also be the key players in any process of change as they are the ones who have to identify and address the causes of the problems. Without their positive contribution the problems of today cannot be addressed, nor will damaging practices be reversed and remedied. Fundamental and much needed change can only be achieved with the integral support and co-operation of those who survey these buildings.

That is why it is imperative that those who encounter the existing building stock in their everyday work are made aware of their responsibility, to manage what is a valuable and finite resource, in a sustainable manner. Property professionals have a duty of care not to ignore the problems of sustainability that this and future generations face. It will only be through their positive contribution that we will be able to pass on what we have in a sound and maintainable condition.

> In the same way that the building regulations are accepted without question in the design and running of our buildings, we must build in the same good quality practice for environmental matters. It shouldn't be left as an issue for the environmentalists, but a matter of course that is part of the normal advice procedures of a professional person. So if we give advice that excludes environmental concerns, it should be the case that we could be liable for negligence. We must bring the knowledge and thought processes that go with sustainable development into the comfort zone of the professional adviser.
>
> Peter Fall, RICS President.[9]

References

1 McIntosh, A., *Soil and Soul: People versus corporate power*, London, 2001, p. 210.

2 Oxley, R., 'Thinking of surveying an historic building?', *CSM (Chartered Surveyor Monthly)* January 1997, p. 41.

3 Curwell, S., Fox, B., Greenberg, M., and March, C., *Hazardous Building Materials: A guide to the selection of environmentally responsible alternatives*, Second Edition, Spon Press, London, 2002.

4 *Toxic Treatments: Wood preservative hazards at work and in the home*, London Hazards Centre, London, 1988.

5 *Digest 299 Dry rot: Its recognition and control*, Building Research Establishment, July 1985.

6 *English House Condition Survey 1996*, DETR (Department of the Environment, Transport and the Regions), 1998.

7 *The Stirling Charter*, Historic Scotland, 2000.

8 Woolley, T., Kimmins, S., Harrison, P and Harrison, R., *Green Building Handbook, Volume 1: A guide to building products and their impact on the environment*, Spon Press, London, 2001, p. 10.

9 Fall, P., *RICS Business* (The Magazine of the Royal Institution of Chartered Surveyors), October 2002, p. 16.

THE NEED FOR CHANGE

As sustainable management is holistic in approach, it is important that areas of potential conflict are identified and addressed.[1]

INFLUENCE OF EXTERNAL FACTORS

This chapter examines the external influences that can lead to inappropriate and damaging work to traditional buildings. Such an examination is crucial to understanding the external factors that influence how practitioners approach and report on traditional buildings, and is necessary if we are to understand the root of the problems and implement effective change.

The manner in which many property professionals inspect, survey, report and specify is dictated by external factors, as they have to conform to and satisfy certain standards and requirements. Professional practice is therefore strongly influenced by a complex relationship between the institutions, such as the RICS (Royal Institution of Chartered Surveyors) and the RIBA (Royal Institute of British Architects), their members, their clients, consumer pressure and the risks of negligence.

Certain practices, some of which are examined below, have become commonplace and are accepted as the norm as they conform to preconceived expectations. They are a response to the pressures and demands that result in a standardised approach, one that actually restricts the practitioner's ability to react to highly individual situations in an appropriate and sympathetic way.

Case Study 2.1 Report standardisation

This case is typical of how questions asked of the inspecting practitioner can increase the risk of a building being exposed to unnecessary and damaging work. In this case a mortgage lender poses the following question in a risk assessment report:

Is there dry rot?

A box is provided for the valuer to answer yes or no.

If the question is affirmative the valuer is encouraged to make a recommendation, by selecting from a menu of standard paragraphs including the following:

1. There are signs of serious rot and repairs may be expensive. You now need a specialist to check thoroughly all the timbers to identify the extent of the problem and give you a quotation for all the necessary repairs.
2. There is evidence of dampness to ground floor walls and timbers in contact may be defective. You should instruct a specialist contractor to investigate the full extent and carry out necessary repair work.

At face value these paragraphs appear sound. However, closer scrutiny of the likely consequences of acting on this advice suggests otherwise. The question asked demands an answer that cannot be always answered correctly or concisely.[2] The principal reason being that it is not always possible to make a positive diagnosis of dry rot (*Serpula lacrymans*) from a visual non-destructive inspection unless there is an archetypal fruit body or other growth characteristic present.

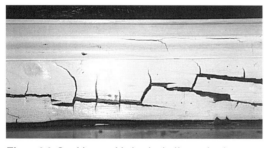

Figure 2.1 Cracking to skirting is similar to the damage characteristics of dry rot. But is it dry rot?

Is the damage shown in figure 2.1 above dry rot? Yes or no?

It meets the description of the damage characteristics of dry rot of deep cracks along and across the grain. On the evidence available it would be reasonable to expect that dry rot is present.

But the removal of the skirting and adjacent timbers reveals brown/black strands, which are a characteristic of cellar fungus (*Coniophora puteana*) not dry rot.[3] This level of inspection would not be possible in most inspections for valuation or survey.

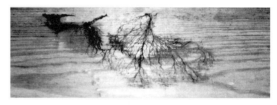

Figure 2.2 Further investigations reveals brown/black strands, characteristic of cellar fungus not dry rot.

However, the practitioner has been asked to make a positive decision as to whether or not the timber decay is dry rot. This will in many cases be impossible to achieve from a visual non-destructive inspection alone. Irrespective of these difficulties the practitioner still has to respond to the question by answering either yes or no. This leaves little or no room for manoeuvre. What is the result of such a question?

If in doubt the practitioner will in many cases veer naturally towards caution and ask by means of a standard paragraph for a specialist report. This is because the practitioner has limited time or opportunity for diagnosis and has to respond within the confines of the report format. This will inevitably result in the building being inspected by a specialist contractor with a vested financial interest in their own recommendations.

The limitations of the inspection, the standardisation of the inspection report form, and the restrictions this places on the manner of reporting create a situation that, invariably, leads to unnecessary work.

In this case it is not necessarily the practitioner who is at fault, it is the process within which the practitioner has to work that needs modification.

This example illustrates that the individual characteristics of many traditional buildings make them particularly vulnerable to the inflexibility of standardised processes and systems, which in many cases are deeply flawed and contribute significantly to the practitioner response. In many situations the practitioner is forced into providing advice or recommendations that are not necessarily appropriate for the building in question. This is potentially damaging to the building and to the reputation of property professionals.

PROTECTION

We have, as a society, identified a group of buildings as being culturally important, as deserving statutory protection to assist in their protection and preservation – such as those buildings that are listed or situated in conservation areas. As a result, buildings that do not fall within this categorisation become more vulnerable than those that are protected. No matter how interesting and valuable they may be, buildings that are not protected are seen as having no special value, and this is often reflected in how many of these buildings are treated.

Figure 2.3 A building that is not listed or is not situated in a conservation area is more likely to be subject to inappropriate intervention.

Even where the protection of legislation is in place, it is put to the test on a daily basis. There is a culture of resistance to authority. This is reflected in the extent and nature of unauthorised works that have been successfully prosecuted, examples of which are illustrated below:[4]

- the construction of unauthorised extensions and alterations
- alterations made to roofs; replacement of roof coverings, installation of skylights

- removal of cast iron guttering; replacement with pvc guttering
- removal of windows
- replacement of timber sash windows with uPVC windows
- installation of concrete lintels
- removal of chimney stacks and chimney breasts
- demolition of buildings and outbuildings
- alterations to curtilage buildings
- removal of entrance gates
- removal of statues
- removal and installation of shop fronts
- cement rendering of external brickwork
- painting external brickwork
- making holes in walls to insert extractor fans
- internal alterations; removal of plasterwork, internal panelling, doors, fireplaces, ceiling mouldings, architraves, skirtings, partitions and chimney breasts
- sand blasting of timbers
- lowering cellar floor
- destruction of redundant and working mill machinery

The loss of fabric and the resultant erosion of character, in many instances simply for short-term economic gain, threatens the very significance that made these buildings worthy of protection in the first place. As Nicholas Hawksmoor noted in the eighteenth century:

> Whatever is good in its kinde ought to be preserv'd in respect for antiquity, as well as our present advantage, for destruction can be profitable to none but such as live by it.[5]

Clearly the challenges of today have their roots in the past.

Unauthorised changes may also be detrimental to the building or the environment. Fabric that has a serviceable life is often removed and replaced with products that do not have the same proven longevity.

> Faulty judgements arise from ignorance of the availability of crafts and materials, the desire to find cheap and easy solutions and the belief that modern methods are, in any case, superior to traditional materials.[6]

The replacement of existing fabric with modern materials is unfortunately a common response, as repair is often perceived to be inferior. Where the practitioner also believes this to be the case the pressure to use replacement materials will increase.

BETTERMENT AND WELL-MARKETED PRODUCTS

One of the most significant external pressures influencing how buildings are repaired, maintained and modernised, comes from the plethora of lifestyle magazines and television programmes concerned with home improvement.

We are encouraged to spend money on our buildings, with the implicit promise that the results will improve self-esteem and enhance how we are regarded by others. This is not a new phenomenon, similar examples can be seen throughout history. The difference today is that a greater number of people are exposed to a powerful media and active marketing. These exceptional circumstances are creating potentially serious problems for the future. The availability of well-marketed and relatively cheap products feed the desire and opportunity for widespread home 'improvement'. This has brought considerable pressure to bear on the existing building stock, particularly where there is an emphasis on replacement rather than repair such as in the case of the installation of uPVC windows.

New products are being introduced at a rate never experienced before. They are promoted and marketed as being good and beneficial, and in some cases they are perceived as increasing the financial value of the building. Often materials are promoted as providing simple solutions to what are in reality highly complex problems. In many cases the solutions advocated may be appropriate for conventional modern buildings, but may not provide the correct remedy for older buildings, for example masonry paints and water repellent coatings.

MODERN EXPECTATIONS AND DEMANDS

In many ways, modern expectations are incompatible with the limitations of the traditional building stock. Buildings are expected to meet certain standards, and to meet our minimum requirements. We expect modern homes to be dry and warm; to have smooth finishes to the walls; for a house to have two bathrooms, preferably one en-suite; for commercial premises to have air conditioning or lifts.

Legislative requirements may impose demands and expectations that conflict with the interests of the building, or which the building may not be able to accommodate; for instance, the requirement to improve access arrangements in public buildings for those with disabilities.[7] Although there are measures in place to prevent any unreasonable physical changes that legislation may inflict on existing buildings, a pressure for change has been created.

The problem is that many existing buildings cannot meet these demands and expectations. This may be because the building is listed, the building has been damp for centuries and cannot be dried out quickly to modern comfort levels, or it is very draughty and cannot be heated effectively, or it is too small to provide all the amenities that modern living demands.

These demands create a pressure for instant one-off solutions to what may be either complex and long-standing problems, or just perceived problems. Probably the most commonly encountered examples are the demands made for damp and timber treatment, with pressure to treat all exposed timbers. This wholesale application of preservatives can rarely be justified, and is likely to be contrary to current legislation.[8] However, irrespective of the controls in place, wholesale treatment still continues in order to meet demand and expectations, and has become accepted to some extent as an industry standard.

WARRANTIES AND GUARANTEES

An example of what has become an industry standard is the expectation for new build and conversions to have a guarantee of warranty against serious structural problems. For example, the NHBC (National House-Building Council) offers a ten-year warranty that protects buyers of new homes against specified defects if the building fails to comply with the NHBC Standards.[9] The influence that such a scheme can have on an existing building is illustrated in the case study below.

Case Study 2.2 Cavity wall corrosion

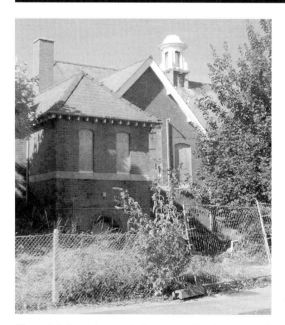

Figure 2.4 An early twentieth-century school constructed in cavity brickwork.

Although the building in this case study is not of a traditional construction it illustrates the invisible pressures that influence how a building is repaired and altered. It also offers an insight into some of the issues relating to other forms of construction, as it is rare to find a building that has not been altered or extended during its history.

This case involved a school constructed in 1909 that was being converted into apartments and flats. The school is unlisted but is one of the focal buildings within a conservation area. The building is an early form of cavity construction comprising the original 1909 core and later 1930 additions (figure 2.4).

The builder was required to replace the cavity wall ties so that the conversion would obtain a ten-year warranty. To achieve this it was proposed that the outer skin of brickwork should be removed and rebuilt to match the existing style, as this would allow the cavity wall ties to be replaced. This approach was based on the findings of a report produced by a company that specialised in cavity wall replacement.

The conservation officer had serious reservations concerning how this proposal would affect the character of the building and asked for an independent report on the condition of the wall ties, to determine if they needed replacement and whether or not the walls had to be rebuilt. An examination of the literature available on cavity wall ties, and its application to the building in question, revealed the following:

The justification for the replacement of cavity wall ties is usually based upon interpretation of selected information. Unfortunately there is a perception that the corrosion of cavity wall ties is a serious and widespread problem, and as a result, they are widely condemned. This can be traced back to interpretation of research from the Building Research Establishment (BRE) that has shown that steel ties made before 1981 could corrode prematurely and that wall tie corrosion is a very widespread defect, potentially affecting about 10 million UK dwellings.[10] This statement has been applied in a general manner and is not necessarily applicable to early forms of cavity construction. Examination of other information available from the BRE puts the statement into perspective.

The BRE state that most masonry buildings are sufficiently robust to accommodate the effects of corrosion of ties although some remedial work may be necessary eventually. Nevertheless, the effects of corrosion are likely to be more significant in certain high rise and cross-wall buildings.[11] The building in question, because of its age, was neither high rise nor cross wall construction.

The earliest metal ties were fabricated from wrought and cast iron and have generally, but not invariably performed satisfactorily.[12] The BRE has identified that in buildings constructed before 1945 the wall ties were galvanised. The quality of coating may have been as good as subsequent standards as wall ties from this period have been shown to have two to three times the minimum weight of galvanised coating.[13]

Virtually all pre-1945 masonry buildings with cavity walls are likely to be of a cellular building type and most of these contain vertical-twist ties, in which case corrosion and the possible need for remedial work should become apparent from the disruption of mortar beds well in advance of any failure of the outer leaf. The structural form of a cellular building should ensure continued stability. The BRE states that the outer leaves could fail ultimately by bowing outwards, but the vertical loads would continue to be supported by the inner leaves which are buttressed by intersecting walls. Consequently, early detection of corrosion is not crucial. Walls in which the majority of ties have corroded would be more susceptible to loading imposed by strong winds.[14]

When assessing a building, the areas at greatest risk need to be inspected. 'Collapses of walls or parts of walls, especially at the heads of gables, due to wind suction in gale conditions, occur occasionally.'[15] This made the assessment of the gables at the school a priority so that the condition of the wall ties and the risks of failure could be determined. In this case the pointing to the south-facing gables was badly weathered and the re-building of the gables could be justified.

Most existing buildings are of a cellular plan form and, though corrosion of wall ties may lead to some reduction in the strength of the walls, widespread problems are unlikely. Where vertical-twist ties have been used, horizontal cracking should reveal the existence of corrosion sufficiently early to enable appropriate action to be taken.[16]

In this case there was no evidence of horizontal cracking to indicate any serious corrosion of the cavity wall ties.

Galvanised ties with a white deposit or encrustation ('white rust') or a blackening of the zinc coating are showing evidence of zinc corrosion. Ties showing evidence of red rust either in the section within the cavity or where they are embedded in the mortar, are already in an advanced state of deterioration and will sooner or later fail. Ties not showing signs of red rust may be examined by metallurgical or chemical analysis methods given in BS 729 and BS 2989 to establish the remaining zinc thickness, and their remaining life may then be estimated.

If no evidence of corrosion exists or a reasonable life is estimated, then the minimum action should be to note the dwellings for future inspection.[17]

An inspection of the exposed ties was made to assess their condition (figure 2.5). The findings were noted and a recommendation made for metallurgical or chemical analysis. Ties suffering from 'zinc light corrosion' have a predicted life of greater than twenty-five years and no action is required, and ties suffering from 'zinc white rust' have a predicted life of greater than ten years and require an inspection between 5–10 years.[18] The condition of the wall ties at the school was such that they would be expected to have a life beyond a ten-year warranty.

This case study illustrates that condemning cavity wall ties on the basis of a selected statement, whilst ignoring the other relevant information available, does not result in reasoned and informed decisions. Unfortunately, accepted common practice is all too often based upon unjustified or partially justified generalisations.

In this case a compromise was found and the external skin was retained. However, in order to obtain a warranty, new ties were drilled between the inner and outer leaves of the internal face from the building. This solution prevented damage to the narrow mortar joints to the external skin of brickwork, but, it could be argued, was not required for the health of the majority of the building. Nevertheless, the compromise did satisfy all concerned.

This case typifies many instances where remedial works become an industry standard that can be implemented without questioning. By questioning the standard approach a considerable amount of time and money was saved by the builder and as a consequence the demand for new bricks, the drain on resources and the embodied energy this would have involved, were also significantly reduced, meaning they achieved a far more environmentally conscious solution.

Figure 2.5 An exposed cavity tie.

The demand for a quick fix is often coupled with the requirement for works to be backed by guarantees. This can result in over-specification in order to reduce the risk of a claim on the guarantee. Work undertaken to meet these increasing standards, is not always necessary or appropriate, and moves us further away from doing what is right for many traditional buildings.

A guarantee for damp or timber treatment will invariably state that it will be invalidated if the building has not been well maintained, even though in most cases a well-maintained building would not require damp or timber treatment, thereby negating the need for a guarantee in the first place. In many cases property professionals, banks and building societies and property owners drive the demand for guarantees, based upon the desire for a single instant solution. More often than not such a solution does not exist, but the benefit of a guarantee gives credibility in many cases to what are, when examined closely, spurious practices, such as those illustrated in Case Studies 1.2 and 8.1.

Change and improvement should be based on informed and reasoned decisions that are not for short-term gain or detrimental to the building. There needs to be increased awareness that, in the case of many traditional buildings, the introduction of cement-based pointing and renders, modern masonry paints, damp-proof courses, and waterproofing sealants will only increase the risks of damp and decay.

Many modern products used in the repair of buildings can, when used in isolation or when applied to a stable background, meet the stated performance. But problems can be experienced where these materials are used on older buildings, as they can be found to be incompatible with the fabric that they are applied to. A modern product is likely to be introduced only because there is a problem, or where there is a perceived need to carry out a repair. However, in many cases, the existing building fabric is likely to be unstable, and the introduction of a new material with different performance characteristics can exacerbate the situation, possibly accelerating the rate of deterioration.

It would be wise to stop and ask the following before starting work: Is the building capable of meeting the demands and expectations placed upon it, without prejudicing its condition, serviceability and longevity?

AN ACTIVE PROPERTY MARKET

The demands for betterment and increased expectations can be compounded when a building is subjected to the whims and desires of several owners over a relatively short period of time. An active and transient property market, as experienced in the last thirty years or so, may result in some buildings having a new owner as often as every three to five years. This will take its toll, as each owner tries to stamp their personality on the building by carrying out a range of repairs and improvements. Often any surviving authentic fabric will be eroded away by the damaging actions of a succession of well intentioned owners.

Eventually, one of the owners will want to reinstate the building back to its original state. The fireplaces removed are now considered desirable and therefore valuable – they are a positive selling point. The building may be subjected to a conjectural restoration in an attempt to reinstate its authenticity. Unfortunately the historic fabric – the windows, the fireplaces, doors and skirtings, are all lost – they are irreplaceable; only modern equivalents or salvaged materials can be used to replace the materials. The demand for authentic salvaged materials and features now puts additional pressure on the remainder of the existing building stock, as

Figure 2.6 The balcony and verandah provide the principal character features of this building. The loss of these features would remove the interest that has survived.

Figure 2.7 (left) This building retains little, if any redeeming features. The windows and shop front are all modern. The pebbledash render is modern and is inappropriate in appearance and performance.

Figure 2.8 (right) A pair of impressive doors. Alteration or replacement of either one of the doors would change not only the appearance of the building but also affect the character of its neighbour.

other buildings are stripped of their materials to be reinstated, probably inappropriately, for the 'restoration'. This creates a vicious cycle that compounds the dilution of authenticity of more buildings.

The practitioner can play an important role in reducing the demands made on buildings, by educating and increasing the awareness of the owners and potential purchasers as to the value of the fabric, which materials are appropriate, and if necessary, advising the client that they should not be buying that building at all. Changes made to meet short-term economic gains are not necessarily the best long-term solutions and are invariably not the only option.

INDIVIDUALITY VERSUS STANDARDISATION

The whole process of standardisation is now endemic throughout the building process, from the choice of materials available, the methods of repair and maintenance, training and education, through to the responses of property professionals to situations that they encounter in their everyday work.

The diverse nature of the existing building stock is diminishing rapidly, as local practices and traditions are being lost and mass-produced and well-marketed products replace traditional materials, for example, masonry paint is now commonplace, whereas the use of limewash is a rarity. A reliance on modern products has resulted in a loss of cultural confidence, an acceptance without questioning the inauthentic, the inappropriate, and the damaging.

Many older buildings are vernacular; they can be readily identified as being of a certain time and belonging to a particular environment, region or locality. A greater emphasis on the use of traditional materials would improve the condition and longevity of older buildings, it would also reinstate the physical association with the land from which these buildings are derived. As Clifton-Taylor eloquently writes:

> But usually no materials look as well as the local ones, which belong organically to their landscape, harmonize with neighbouring buildings and nearly always give the best colours. There are still many old houses scattered over our countryside which convey the impression of having grown out of the soil untouched by the hand or mind of Man.[19]

Vernacular buildings by their very nature reflect the materials of their immediate locality. The use of mass-produced materials to alter, repair and maintain these buildings has considerably diluted the link between these structures and their surrounding environment. In many cases there is no longer a living link with someone who has the knowledge and skills to understand how these buildings should be repaired, maintained or even presented.

There is a need for diversity in the built environment that reflects the long tradition of a locality, a region, and even a nation, that has developed over time to meet and adjust to highly individual social and environmental circumstances. Without diversity we are left with a monoculture, which in itself creates pressure to conform to what is inauthentic. The more that our knowledge and appreciation of traditional methods and values is diluted the more likely it is that we cannot look at what we have got and understand what is wrong. We end up suffering from cultural amnesia.

Case Study 2.3 **Reinstating limewash**

In this case some local residents questioned the application of a traditional limewash finish in a recently completed programme of repair, as it did not conform to the conventionally accepted presentation of a timber-framed building.

The work to the building in question included the removal of inappropriate impervious cement renders to the infill panels, repair of the surviving wattle and daub and lime render infill panels, reinstatement of appropriate and compatible earth and lime-based renders, and provision of a traditional limewash finish.

The use of modern impervious materials in past programmes of repair was preventing the building from performing as originally intended. The impervious cement renders and modern masonry paints were impairing the ability of moisture to evaporate from the building and this increased the risks of decay to the structural timber frame. The principal aim of the programme of repair work was to remove the inappropriate cement renders and modern paints and to reinstate the 'breathing' performance using traditional materials and methods that would allow the building to be passed on to future generations in a sound and maintainable condition.

The conservation officer received comments questioning the application of a yellow ochre limewash over the timber frame and infill panels. These objections arose because the majority of historic timber-framed buildings are now presented as black and white, with the timbers clearly picked out from the infill panels. This presentation of timber-framed buildings is, in many cases, a Victorian or Edwardian perception of how these buildings should be presented – a response to some buildings being traditionally 'painted' black and white and also the fashion for the 'Mock-Tudor' around the turn of the twentieth century. Unfortunately, the removal or concealment of historic finishes, and painting timber-framed buildings black and white, has become common practice and resulted in the erosion over the years of regional differences in the presentation of these buildings as well as their traditional performance.

In this case, photographic evidence shows the neighbouring building was fully rendered in the

Figure 2.9 Photograph taken in the 1920s showing part of the building rendered. The gable on the far left is decorated with a 'Star of David', lost when the render was removed.

Figure 2.10 The same building repaired and limewashed.

Figure 2.11 Detail of the building repaired. The limewash has improved the weathering capabilities.

1920s (figure 2.9). The timber frame to this building was never meant to be exposed. The removal of the render not only removed a protective finish but also a decorative one, a 'Star of David', which was also known as the 'Seal of Solomon' and the 'Shield of David'. The relevance of this symbol and what it represented, its significance and the manner in which older buildings were presented and decorated, are not clearly understood. In this case this information has been lost forever, reflecting the need to prevent the loss of historic fabric, as we still are rediscovering the past.

Unfortunately, the reinstatement of traditional finishes, such as limewash, is the exception rather than the norm, despite the fact that limewashing is appropriate and compatible and in the building's long-term interest. The decision to limewash the external elevations was based upon a reasoned and informed decision gained from an understanding of the building, and other buildings of a similar age and type of construction, in particular the original performance and likely presentation.

Practical reasons for limewashing:

- it allows the building to perform as originally intended – as a breathing structure
- it provides the maximum protection to the historic fabric – particularly to the gaps between the infill panels and the timbers that are vulnerable
- limewashing of the oriel window and bargeboard to the north gable provided a unified scheme to the repairs (figure 2.11)
- the limewash provides improved protection to the timbers where it fills existing crevices and joints that can be exploited by the weather
- the limewash significantly improves the protection against weathering and decay and will therefore slow down the rates of deterioration

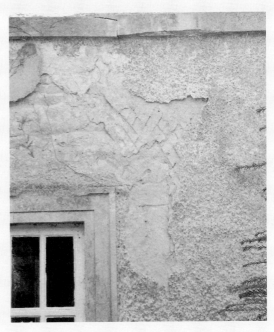

Figures 2.12a and 2.12b This building is currently part rendered and part exposed rubble stonework. The rubble stonework was never intended to be seen, it was concealed from view and protected from the elements by a decorative render – with quoins and ornate window detailing – all in a lime render. The render has failed or been removed over time. Unfortunately, the removal of render from many stone buildings has resulted in a loss of continuity of traditional presentation, and it is now considered as correct to view rubble stonework. If either the owner who commissioned the original construction of the building, or the builder, were alive to see the exposed rubble, they would be horrified at the loss of the decorative and protective render, as the stone was seen as a cheap and rough material.

EDUCATION AND TRAINING

Practitioners are taught primarily how individual constructional elements of a building are put together, but of equal importance is the interrelationship between different components, and the consequences of changes that the introduction of new materials can have on an existing building.

Education and training relating to older, and in particular historic, buildings has been severely limited until relatively recently. Even now the education and training of many property professionals, primarily architects and surveyors, does not include a satisfactory introduction to the differences between traditional and modern methods of construction, and there is little or no positive instruction on how to survey older buildings. For example, a commonly perceived defect is that of dampness, yet there is very little training in diagnosing damp problems, nor is there mandatory training of property professionals on how to use a moisture meter – just that they should use one. The current system does not produce a sufficient number of professionals with the necessary skills, nor does it encourage them to act as good custodians.

The areas where the education and training of professionals can be improved include an understanding of:

- the materials and methods of construction of traditional buildings
- the performance characteristics of the materials used to build and repair traditional buildings
- the dynamics of air and moisture movement in a building and its relationship with the external environment
- the consequences of any changes in the intended performance of traditional buildings
- the materials and methods of repair and maintenance appropriate for traditional buildings

PROFESSIONAL GUIDANCE

The institutions representing property professionals have generally undervalued the importance of building conservation. This is reflected in the limited amount of literature produced by the institutions for their members written specifically for the inspection and survey of historic and traditional buildings. This weakness contributes to the lack of awareness of the distinctive characteristics of traditional buildings and how to take account of them. Consequently, guidelines are not yet included in standard practice, many property professionals encounter traditional buildings totally unprepared, and are therefore incapable of offering appropriate advice and recommendations.

The Chartered Institution of Building Services Engineers (CIBSE) has produced an important publication, *Guide to Building Services for Historic buildings*,[20] that provides positive advice on the performance of traditional buildings, practical guidance relating to building services in traditional buildings, as well as aiming to make a sustainable approach to historic and traditional buildings an everyday activity, rather than the exception to the rule. Unfortunately, similar guidance from other institutions is sadly lacking. Other information that is applicable to older buildings is primarily concerned with the valuation of buildings, and can be found in the RICS (Royal Institution of Chartered Surveyors) *Appraisal and Valuation Standards* (the 'Red Book') and TEGoVA's (The European Group of Valuers' Associations) *European Valuation Standards* (the 'Blue Book') (see Appendices 1 and 2).

In November 2002 the final draft of the RICS Guidance Notes for the Residential Building Survey included the following:

5.1 Constructional Principles

It should be made clear to the client that older buildings were constructed differently, the materials and methods of construction being different from those of modern buildings – consequently older buildings will perform differently. This section is therefore not just applicable to 'historic' buildings but to all buildings of a traditional type.

Works causing changes in the intended performance of a traditional building can have detrimental consequences on its condition; for example the entrapment of moisture by impervious materials used in repair and maintenance such as cement-based renders, pointing, plasters and modern paints. Understanding how a building was constructed and intended to perform and any changes to that performance are fundamental to successfully determining a building's existing and future condition. The 'breathing' performance is important to all traditional buildings and the surveyor should make full use of this section in order that an assessment of the intended and existing performance can be made and the issues explained to the client.[21]

This provides clear guidance to the practitioner that there is a fundamental difference between traditional and modern buildings, and that any changes in the intended performance can have detrimental consequences. It will take some time for the benefits of this guidance, if adopted, to be realised but it is a significant step in the right direction, and is guidance that will be applicable to the mainstream not just those practitioners who specialise in the survey of historic buildings.

PROFESSIONAL INDEMNITY INSURANCE AND NEGLIGENCE

Every property professional will only be too aware that the risk of charges of negligence is one of the most influential factors dictating the manner in which they inspect and report. Property professionals mitigate these risks by taking out professional indemnity insurance as cover against financial loss as a consequence of a negligence action.

The pressure of potential negligence, and the financial repercussions of increased insurance premiums and excesses, creates a climate of fear that naturally results in defensive reporting. This is reflected in the standardisation of reports, which are full of negative caveats and carefully worded phrases. Practitioners, as a result, often relinquish their responsibility to third parties, although where this occurs it is not uncommon to find that the person asked to comment is less qualified than the inspecting practitioner who made the initial survey, and have a vested financial interest in the recommendations that they make (Chapter 8).

The application of standard solutions, derived from standard clauses, to what are non-standard buildings only perpetuates what can be seen to be a highly destructive process. Paradoxically, the use of standard clauses for situations typically encountered when surveying highly individual buildings only increases the risk of negligence. The most effective way for practitioners to defend themselves against potential negligence claims is by reflecting the differences between traditional and modern buildings in their surveys and by avoiding the application of standard phrases, recommendations and specifications to buildings that are, more often than not, unique.

As can be seen, the influence of external factors is fundamental to how traditional buildings are surveyed and repaired. Our challenge now is how to overcome deep-rooted practices. The over-riding need for change should provide sufficient justification to address this.

References

1 'Managing the historic environment sustainably', *Passed to the Future: Historic Scotland's Policy for the Sustainable Management of the Historic Environment*, Historic Scotland, 2002, p. 14.

2 Oxley, R., 'Valuing and Surveying Historic Buildings – The Future', *Journal of Architectural Conservation*, Vol. 5, No. 3, November 1999, pp. 44–5.

3 Bravery, A.F., Berry, R.W., Carey, J.K. and Cooper, D.E., *Recognising Wood Rot and Insect Damage in Buildings*, Building Research Establishment, 1992.

4 Kindred, B., *The National Database of Listed Building Prosecutions*, this document is maintained for the Institute of Historic Building Conservation by Bob Kindred MBE (Appendix 4).

5   Hawksmoor, Nicholas, Letter to Dr George Clarke, Fellow of All Souls Oxford (on the rebuilding of the College), 17 February 1715.

6   Earl, J., *Building Conservation Philosophy*, Third Edition, Donhead Publishing, Shaftesbury, 2003, p. 94

7   Disability Discrimination Act, 1995.

8   Control of Substances Hazardous to Health Regulations, 1988.

9   NHBC (National House Building Council) website: www.nhbc.co.uk

10 *Good Repair Guide 4: Replacing masonry wall ties*, Building Research Establishment (BRE), December 1996.

11 'Introduction', *BRE Current Paper 3/81: Performance of Cavity Wall Ties*, April 1981.

12 'Introduction', *BRE Information Paper 12/90: Corrosion of Steel Wall Ties: history of occurrence, background and treatment*, November 1990.

13 'Age and type of tie (Existing Buildings)', *BRE Current Paper 3/81 Performance of Cavity Wall Ties*, April 1981, p. 15, 4.1.

14 'Possible consequences (Existing Buildings)', *BRE Current Paper 3/81 Performance of Cavity Wall Ties*, April 1981, p. 17, 4.4.

15 'Assessment and Action', *BRE information paper 12/90: Corrosion of Steel Wall Ties: history of occurrence, background and treatment*, November 1990.

16 'Conclusions', *BRE Current Paper 3/81: Performance of Cavity Wall Ties*, p.19, and *BRE Information Paper 4/81: The performance of Cavity Wall Ties*, April 1981.

17 *BRE Information Paper 12/90*, November 1990.

18 *BRE Digest 401*, January 1995.

19 Clifton-Taylor, A., *The Pattern of English Building*, Fourth Edition, Faber & Faber, London, 1987, pp. 23–4.

20 David, J. (ed.), *Guide to Building Services for Historic Buildings*, The Chartered Institution of Building Services Engineers, London, 2002.

21 RICS Residential Building Survey Guidance Notes, final draft, December 2002.

3 | VALUES AND PRINCIPLES

Whatever motives society may have for preserving old buildings and whatever legislative and other controls may be available, preservation is ultimately, in the most literal sense, in the hands of the building professions and crafts people. The most pressing philosophical questions must, therefore, be concerned with practice.[1]

The factors that need to be taken into account when surveying or repairing a traditional building can be derived largely from the philosophical approach and from principles developed in the field of building conservation. Whether building conservation is relevant to unlisted buildings will undoubtedly be questioned, as it is probably the case that only those that are listed are considered worthy of conservation at present, but a truly sustainable approach will only be achieved if based upon a reasoned and informed approach that is applied to as many buildings as possible. There is a need to be inclusive, so that good practice is applied generally, and not just to those buildings that are protected.

DEFINING SPECIAL INTEREST

An older building can have a 'value' that a modern building will not yet have obtained. This 'value' can be described as the special interest of a building. Each individual building will have particular qualities that contribute to this interest; these may be attributable to age, type, method of construction, style, or an association with famous people, events or designing architect (refer to Chapter 6 Legislation).

Any damage or loss of fabric will act to devalue or detract from the interest of a building, and the loss of a building itself will dilute the character and appeal of its surrounding environment.

It is therefore critical for the practitioner to be able to clearly identify the special interest of a building and its fabric. Only then can advice or recommendations be made without the practitioner unwittingly contributing to damage or loss that will undermine its interest or value.

Perhaps the greatest mental hurdle in accepting the 'conservation' approach is the emphasis placed on saving what may seem an ordinary or even worthless part of the fabric. It is easy to appreciate the quality of an intricately moulded seventeenth-century plaster ceiling or an Adam fireplace, but the value of a lime-washed wall, a joist, or the particular thickness of a window astragal is far less obvious. Their importance lies not in their instant visual appeal or even, necessarily, their age, but in their contribution to the value of the whole – a perhaps small but very important part of the building's authenticity as a piece of architecture. Firstly, architecture is much more than an attractive scene-set, it has depth, strength and age, and every original detail, texture, proportion and space is essential to and inextricable from the quality and integrity of the design. Secondly, these less noticeable parts also have a value in themselves. Just as archaeologists now learn as much if not more from the 'debris' of long-gone civilisations as from any buried treasure, so the less 'attractive' parts of buildings have much to tell our own and future generations. The value of the architectural past comes not only from the painting, gilding and carving on show in the state rooms of the rich and powerful but from the unobtrusive signs of everyday labour, for example, the cutting and jointing of timber, the pointing of stone, and the very careful positioning of vents and openings.[2]

Figure 3.1 (left) The neglect, the influence of weathering and a history of alteration and adaptation of this ruin all create a value and interest that is difficult to define.

Figure 3.2 (right) A smoking shed in a seaside town – used for smoking fish. This is the only known survivor in this town of what was once a common feature. The scarcity of this simple structure places a greater 'value' on its survival.

The inspecting practitioner needs to be aware that the building may not of itself be of any particular architectural interest; it may be the building's use and association that provides the special value.

Figure 3.3 Shaw's Corner is a National Trust property in Hertfordshire. It is a large detached Grade II* listed building dating from around the turn of the early part of the twentieth century. It can be argued that this building has no particular architectural merit that justifies listing it as being of 'outstanding' interest, but the reason why this particular building is listed Grade II*, and therefore identified as being of particularly great importance to the nation's built heritage, is that George Bernard Shaw lived in the house from 1906 until his death in 1950.

The building has a strong association with Shaw and contains many artefacts, including literature and personal effects, with some rooms remaining much as they were at the time of his death. These factors make it worthy of its listed status, as a building of outstanding importance.

This interest – 'value' – obviously places severe restrictions on the extent and nature of any recommendations for repair or alteration. To ensure that the building remains as it was at the time of Shaw's death, it is imperative that all decisions regarding future works at Shaw's Corner are based upon an appreciation and understanding of the historical context.

Figures 3.4a and 3.4b Superficially this is not an exceptional row of cottages. They are undoubtedly old but do not have any interest that would warrant a listing greater than Grade II, as being of special architectural or historic interest. They are however, listed Grade I and are considered to be of national importance. This is because they contain extensive schemes of secular wall paintings that are recognised as being amongst the most important in England.

The fabric can provide important clues as to the past use and status of a building. For example, carpenters' marks found on many timber-framed buildings inform us of how the frame was assembled, how the building was used, and even the social function and importance of parts of the building. They can also aid an inspection, by indicating where original timbers are missing or whether repairs have been carried out. They can help unravel the past and they can also be attractive and of interest in their own right.

Markings on stonework or timber can indicate what tools and methods the mason or carpenter used; they can also reflect bygone rituals or have a meaning that we currently do not understand. Research can unravel hidden meaning and improve our understanding not only of the building but the way of life and culture of the people who lived in the buildings.

A relatively common symbol that can be found is the daisy wheel (or *Vesica Piscis*).[3] This is a potent Christian symbol, but according to recent research on a significant fifteenth-century timber-framed building in Wales this symbol could also be a constructional reference, based on geometry, that reflects the plan and cross-sections of the building.[4] This research illustrates that we have, up until now, greatly underestimated the level of thought and understanding that went into the actual design and construction of these buildings.

In this case the carpenter's mark, the daisy wheel, was actually lost in the process of repair. The information that this vital clue provided only survived because it was drawn, detailed and videoed. Fortunately this enabled the information that the symbol conveyed to survive, even if it did not survive itself. In many cases it is highly doubtful that sufficient detail would have been recorded to enable the hypothesis and research to be

Figure 3.5 Example of a daisy wheel on a timber lintel over a fireplace.

tested. The information contained and conveyed in even the most simple of fabric cannot be replaced if it is removed.

> The lesson is loud and clear, that we have much to learn from the recording and analysis of all geometrical carvings or images found in historic buildings and that they should be carefully preserved *in situ* where their meaning is the greatest.[5]

Even thatch, which is often seen as a material that can be readily disposed of, can be of great interest, and there are examples where medieval, smoke-blackened thatch has survived over five hundred years. Historic thatch can illustrate the types of crops used for thatching – which is of interest because many of the cereal straws are no longer grown – and can provide a snapshot in time of the varieties of plant used, the development of thatching, the materials used, the type of fixings and the harvesting methods. It is an irreplaceable data bank of information of how we used to live.[6]

Before embarking on any survey the first action that should be taken by the practitioner is to identify the special interest of the building, as this will assist in putting a 'value' on the building and its fabric. Obtaining a copy of the list description of a listed building is a good starting point (see Chapter 6, Legislation), however, the practitioner needs to be aware of the limitations of the list description, as highlighted in the example above. Making a quantifiable assessment will improve understanding and provide a 'feel' for the building that will encourage the practitioner to treat the building and its fabric appropriately.

The practitioner can, by asking some simple questions, achieve a basic understanding of the special interest of the building that is to be surveyed or repaired:

Figures 3.6a and 3.6b
A Grade II listed cottage, dated in the list description as eighteenth century. The smoke-blackened timbers are indicative of medieval hall house, probably sixteenth century or possibly even earlier. The presence of smoke-blackened thatch enabled the building to be readily identifiable as having medieval origins and pre-dating the listed description.

▣ *Is the building protected?*
▣ *Is it a scheduled ancient monument, listed and/or situated in a conservation area?*
If the building is listed obtain a copy of the list description.
Does the list description make any reference to specific parts or
    features of the building?
Is the list description correct?
▣ *What does the practitioner recognise as being special?*
▣ *Contact the local authority's conservation officer, or the Historic Buildings Inspectorate (English Heritage, Historic Scotland, Cadw or the Department of the Environment in Northern Ireland) to determine if they know of the building and have any information that would assist the survey.*

PHILOSOPHY

A rational approach

Acknowledging the difference and value of older buildings creates a need to act in a philosophical and rational manner, to fully consider the implications of ones decisions before acting.

> ...a sound philosophy is not based on a set of immutable rules but on a clear understanding of what, in each instance, conservation is setting out to achieve. Comprehensive knowledge of all the relevant facts will not, of itself, point the way. The practitioner, and this applies not only to those in direct control of works, must develop a critical and self-critical frame of mind, nurturing the ability to proceed from facts by way of logical argument to defensible – if not inevitable – conclusions.[7]

The practitioner needs to have a grasp of the basic fundamental principles that underpin the preservation and conservation of historic buildings, such as those laid out in English Heritage's *Principles of Repair* (see Appendix 5). Without an appreciation or understanding of why we try to protect them, and an ability to apply that knowledge in practice, it is not possible to provide reasoned or informed advice that is in the best interests of the building being surveyed. Nor can we justify arguments for the retention of the remainder of the existing building stock.

> ...whatever your personal role in the conservation processes, remember that, for the time being, the building, the ensemble, the street or the town is under your protection. It is a heavy responsibility and one that had better be faced philosophically.[8]

Founding fathers

Many of the principles applied today in the conservation of historic buildings have their origins in the nineteenth century and have been shaped by the work of the Society for the Protection of Ancient Buildings (SPAB). William Morris, the founder of the SPAB, challenged the damage being caused to the historic fabric of many of Britain's great cathedrals and other buildings, by over zealous architects who were following the Victorian trend of conjectural restoration rather than preservation.

The case for preservation, rather than restoration, was developed during the nineteenth century. John Ruskin's *Seven Lamps of Architecture* laid many of the foundations of the philosophy that is in use today, both in building and environmental conservation. Morris developed Ruskin's theme of sustainability to arrive at the tenet that we are only trustees for future generations.

> These old buildings do not belong to us only ... they have belonged to our forefathers and they will belong to our descendants unless we play them false. They are not ...our property to do as we like with. We are only trustees for those that come after us.[9]

With this in mind we must learn to survey and repair appropriately so that we prevent the unnecessary loss of buildings and fabric.

Changing values

Values and judgements change over time, and a building that is of little interest today may be deemed to be 'worth' considerably more in the future. For this reason, great care needs to be taken not to preclude buildings or fabric that are currently considered to be lacking in particular importance from an appropriate and sympathetic approach.

The present generation continues to reap the benefits of the work by organisations such as the SPAB and the Georgian Group, as well as other Amenity Societies and pressure groups, who have campaigned to prevent the loss of many historic buildings.

Many buildings once viewed as being of no value or worth have been lost in recent history. Such a building was the Adelphi, a large building that fronted onto the River Thames in London. Constructed between 1768–72 by Robert Adam it was demolished in 1937 and we can now only look at the wonder of the design of this building in illustrations.[10] Our attitude would be different today, and the thought of losing this most impressive building would never even cross our minds. If it had survived it would undoubtedly have been listed. What was once undervalued would now be highly prized and appreciated.

Buildings can be lost for many reasons, including economic, social, or political, or as the result of fire. Irrespective of what has caused a building to be lost, it can never be replaced. With hindsight, we may only lament over loss of beauty contained in its fabric and craftsmanship, while its history and character, the reasons for its construction and development are physically removed from the earth and from our memory. Tastes and values change over time, and for this reason great care is needed to avoid the loss or dilution of authenticity, physical loss, or accelerated decay that could prejudice the functional use and enjoyment of buildings by future generations. They may come to place a greater value on them – whether for their architectural or historic merit or because, increasingly importantly, they contain resources that are no longer available.

Figures 3.7a and 3.7b In the 1950s, the action of one man, who objected to plans to demolish a village building to make way for a car park, has proven to be of great value. By purchasing the building and making it his home he saved it from demolition. Whilst it was not valued or understood at the time, it is now Grade II★ listed, being of 'outstanding' architectural or historic interest and of particular importance to the nation's built heritage. This dramatic change of attitude, reflects increased knowledge and appreciation. Research shows that the building dates from the late fourteenth century, with an unusual carving on one of the timbers being of particular interest. A commodity that was seen as disposable is now seen to have great value.

APPROPRIATE REPAIR

One of the fundamental principles behind current building conservation philosophy is to achieve the preservation of the existing building stock by appropriate and careful repair. Putting this into practice can be difficult, particularly as the highly individual nature of older buildings demands that no hard and fast rules can be applied; each building has to be assessed and judged on its own merits and circumstances. In the words of A.R. Powys:

> I have found that it is not wise to lay down dogmatic rules, for when they are made one is apt to be confronted with a case where they do not work.[11]

The adoption of a pragmatic approach, of treating each building on an individual basis, is vital to the successful survey and repair of traditional buildings. The practitioner has to be able to promote solutions that are devised for each circumstance encountered, to move away from a reliance upon standard solutions and those who advocate and profit from them. This principle is reiterated, ironically, in British Standard BS 7913:

> British Standards and other specifications and codes of practice should not be applied unthinkingly, in the context of building conservation. While the application of particular specifications, structural design codes and calculations can be appropriate in many circumstances, there can be other circumstances where it will be necessary to follow professional judgement, on the basis of what has been proved to work.[12]

The practical implication of putting a 'value' on historic buildings and their fabric is that all work should be approached in a conservative manner; with any physical intervention kept to a minimum.[13]

Repair versus replacement

The 'value' of existing fabric dictates that repair should take precedence over replacement, particularly as there is a danger that a succession of replacements may in time erode the fabric, and therefore the character, of a building.

To avoid unnecessary loss it is useful to start with the presumption that all existing fabric is of special interest, that it should always be retained, and it should be subject to the minimum level of repair rather than replacement. Where repair is necessary, the extent can be reduced, with the new repair fitted to the old, rather than adapting the old to accept the new (as illustrated in figure 3.9).

The factors that need to be given careful consideration, even when undertaking what is commonly perceived as a simple task, can be

Case Study 3.1 Inappropriate recommendation

In this case a survey report provided the following recommendation:

> Lath and plaster ceilings can fail without warning and complete renewal in modern plasterboard with modern adequate ceiling joists and binders is considered necessary. We cannot recommend retention of any original lath and plaster ceilings which have now, in our opinion, come to the end of their useful lives.

This defensive reaction to possible failure was not based upon an appreciation that lath and plaster ceilings can be repaired. The nature of the wording suggests it is typical of a standard phrase that may be repeated regularly in building surveys. If this is the case, all lath and plaster ceilings encountered by practitioners using these or similar phrases, may be condemned, and recommendations made for them to be replaced with modern plasterboard because there is a risk of collapse, irrespective of whether or not this is genuinely the case.

The recommendation did not take into account this building's listed status, as no mention was made that listed building consent would be required for the replacement of the lath and plaster ceilings and the joists (refer to Chapter 6,

Legislation). If the recommended works had been carried out without listed building consent the practitioner would have potentially exposed both the prospective new owner and himself to criminal action. It would also have resulted in the irreversible loss of historic fabric.

The maximum retention of historic fabric reduces the demand for replacement materials, in turn reducing the pressures on existing natural resources (see Chapter 4).

Figure 3.8 Is complete stripping out of plaster necessary? Could the plaster have been retained and repaired? If the building is listed, has listed building consent been obtained for the removal of the plaster?

illustrated by using the example of the proposed replacement of some old softwood timber.

> Timber is considered as a building material which can be replaced like for like. If softwood roof timbers are old, with perhaps a few worm holes, then many will consider it sensible and more economical to under take wholesale replacement than to attempt localized repairs. In fact, the old timber removed may have a greater natural durability than any modern replacement, and the slow-grown original, so lightly dismissed, is a vanishing commodity which will soon be irreplaceable.[14]

As slow-grown softwoods are no longer readily commercially available from sustainable sources, greater emphasis needs to be placed on repair rather than wholesale replacement. Society's lack of future planning necessitates that we must now act to put a greater value on both existing and new materials, to be prudent in our management of what we have. We

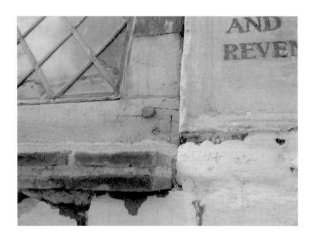

Figure 3.9 Repair of a rotten window frame. The majority of the window frame is retained. Only the rotten sections are replaced with new materials consistent and compatible with the original. This is consistent with good conservation practice.[15]

need to reduce the demands being made on the hardwoods of the rainforests and the softwoods of the Russian tundra, which are a finite resource. The removal of these trees would destroy a means of removing CO_2 from the atmosphere, cause damage to sensitive ecosystems and have an adverse effect on bio-diversity. The demand for materials, and the choices made in building repair, have global consequences. We have to recognise the link between the decisions we make in our everyday context, in the survey and repair of buildings, and safeguarding the future well-being of this planet.

Use of proven materials

In building conservation there is a presumption in favour of the use of traditional materials and methods that are proven to be compatible with the performance of the building. One of the principal benefits of using proven materials and methods is the confidence you can have in the performance of the repair. Conversely it is unwise to experiment with untried materials and techniques, as you can never be confident of the results.

Traditionally, craftsmen had in-depth knowledge and understanding of the characteristics and performance of the materials used to construct and repair buildings. This was primarily due to the passing down of empirical knowledge over years, if not centuries, by the craftsman to his apprentice. The materials available were relatively limited, being primarily masonry, mortars, plasters and timber. These would be tried and tested, and used with confidence.

Today there are thousands of products available that can be used in the construction and repair of buildings, with new products continually coming onto the market and being actively promoted. The difficulty with using these materials in the repair of traditional buildings is that although they will meet some form of standard in their production or short-term performance, their long-term performance and compatibility are unproven.

The testing regimes for new products are unlikely to include all the conditions that can be encountered when in service on an older building. Where the performance of a product has not been tested in real-life conditions it is difficult to have confidence in it, especially when there is an existing pallet of materials to choose from that are proven to be reliable. Nevertheless, the use of modern materials or methods should not be excluded, because in some circumstances they will be necessary to allow the building to be repaired and to continue in beneficial use.

All repairs, and in particular those that rely upon modern materials and methods, need to be carried out with care and with 'reversibility' in mind, so that, where a repair has not remedied the problem or has made it worse, it can be removed without causing any further damage to the building. The use of modern materials, metal straps, wires, glues and resins are illustrated in some of the following case studies.

It is important that each case is assessed upon its own particular circumstances, as a solution suitable for one building may not be appropriate for another.

Case Study 3.2 Metal strap and wire repairs

The outer gable to a Grade II★ listed building is probably an early seventeenth-century addition to a fifteenth-century building, devised to protect the oriel window below.

The outer gable was not fixed adequately at the time it was added to the building and as a result the gable rests on the oriel window. This caused deflection of the window.

Figure 3.10a

Figure 3.10b

The opportunity to provide improved structural restraint and thereby relieve the stresses being exerted on the oriel window arose when carrying out other repairs to the building (see Case Studies 2.3 and 3.4).

Traditional carpentry repairs would have required the gable to be dismantled, but this was not deemed either practical or cost effective, as it would cause severe disruption to other parts of the building to reposition the gable back to its original position.

The repair solution devised in this case was to use metal straps, commonly seen in the repair of historic timber-framed buildings, and steel wires to support and restrain the gable. These repairs achieved the desired aim with the minimal intervention and loss of historic fabric.

Figure 3.11a

Figure 3.11b

The gable was realigned as far as was possible and without causing damage to the building. The opportunity was taken to dismantle and repair the oriel window, as previous repairs using pieced-in timber had weathered badly.

Figure 3.12a

Figure 3.12b

The use of metal straps and wires allowed the repairs to be carried out with the minimum amount of intervention, and in a reversible and honest manner. Although the metal strap and wire repairs are concealed from everyday view a closer inspection would reveal them to be of early twenty-first-century origin.

Developing new skills and techniques

Prior to the development of now accepted and well-established principles for the repair of historic buildings, no cultural value was placed on existing fabric. Decisions were made based on considerations of practicability and cost. If a timber was rotten it would have been replaced. Problems were solved in a pragmatic and practical manner.

In building conservation today it is accepted as good practice to try to retain as much historic fabric as possible; we have put a value on the fabric and make more sophisticated judgements. This automatically changes the way we look at problems and assess the solutions available. Now new techniques are needed – to join new to old, or to halt or slow down decay to fabric that would previously have been replaced.

Traditional repair techniques may also result in unacceptable levels of irreplaceable fabric being lost, such as the cutting of timbers to accommodate a new section. In these circumstances there may be some justification for considering new repair techniques and contemporary, rather than traditional, materials.

The practical conservation of buildings requires innovative skills and ideas that are based upon a new mindset; where different questions are asked and different values and principles applied:

- Can the advice given, or recommendations made, be shown to be strictly necessary?
- Will the recommendations result in the minimal intervention of the historic fabric?
- Will materials and methods be used that are proven to be compatible?
- Are the proposed works reversible?

If all these questions can be answered positively then any advice or recommendations should, in general, be appropriate and sympathetic.

Case Study 3.3 The use of modern repair methods

The Weald and Downland Open Air Museum in Sussex has rescued a number of buildings from destruction; typically buildings threatened by road and rail works and airport expansion. The buildings at the museum have been carefully dismantled, conserved and rebuilt to their original form.

The timber-framed buildings were originally rebuilt and repaired at the museum using traditional carpentry techniques. Over the years dissatisfaction with the appearance and performance of the repair of the external faces of mortices grew. A disproportionate amount of timber had to be cut away to repair a small defect, and the danger of gaps opening up, where the edges of the patch repairs met the old timber, increased the risk of water penetration and further decay. The appearance of the repairs also detracted from the main lines of the frame.[16]

Figure 3.13 The repairs detract from the overall appearance of the building. Gaps between the timbers create areas that can be exploited by water and lead to pockets of damp and decay.

As a result, methods of repair were explored to overcome these problems. The repair methodology developed was based on criteria of cost, performance and minimal disturbance to historic fabric. In addition, the aim was try and make the repairs discreet – not invisible, but not too obvious either – and also to try and make the repairs reflect, in some way, the reasons why they were there.

This led to the development of repair of the mortice faces using both oak and epoxy resin. It is important to appreciate that the use of resins are usually frowned upon in building conservation circles, and as such this was an innovative approach. The repair method devised was as follows.

The timber for the repair was carefully selected to ensure that it had a similar moisture content to the timber being repaired, and converted in a manner, as close as possible to the quarter, to maximise strength. Through various trials a particular epoxy resin was chosen for its qualities as a gap-filling adhesive.

The repair method for the face to the mortices is briefly described below and illustrated in figure 3.14:

1. Consolidate the external face of the damaged area with low viscosity epoxy resin.
2. Cut a slot about 10–12.5 mm wide, leaving about 12.5 mm of the consolidated outer surface. The depth of the slot is dependent on the extent of the defective surface.
3. Cut out the remaining timber between the mortice and the slot.
4. Prepare an oak insert to give a loose push fit.
5. Prime the insert and the slot, and apply epoxy resin as a gap-filling adhesive.
6. Push in the insert, and clamp up the repair.
7. Clean excess resin with tools and/or solvents.

This repair method demands a very high standard of workmanship, and experience of both timber and resin. The museum expects the repairs to be successful but also acknowledges that some may fail, if the epoxy resin bond breaks down.

The museum was able, through the use of this style of repair, to maximise the retention of existing fabric, particularly on the external surfaces where carpenter's markings and weathered surfaces

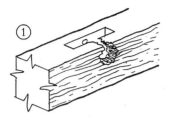

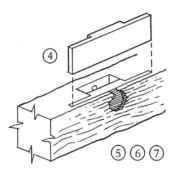

Figure 3.14

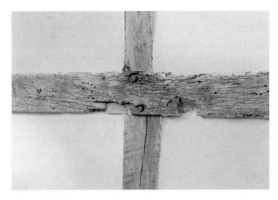

Figure 3.15 Example of an oak and resin repair used in the repair of buildings at the museum. Note how the surfaces of the timbers are retained and provide evidence for the need for repair – in this case decay.

survive. It is these surfaces that can inform and contribute most to the character of a building. The 'internalising' of the repair allowed these surfaces to be retained.

The potential problems associated with the repair of the external faces and mortices – the weathering of joints and interfaces of the timbers – were largely overcome. The repair method was developed and used more extensively in the reconstruction of one of the buildings, Poplar Cottage, at the museum. Knowledge of the performance characteristics of timber, the manner of the repair, and great care being taken in the detailing, avoided the timber-frame being made rigid. The potential problems of condensation, associated with the use of commercially-available resin systems, were also alleviated, although the longer-term performance of the resins, as they are exposed to ultraviolet light, remains unknown.

Where a value has been placed on an older building and its fabric, the approach to repair needs to reflect this. The wholesale replacement or removal of fabric is not acceptable, repairs have to be devised that keep intervention to a minimum; this is not always achievable using traditional methods and materials. New ways of repairing buildings must be developed to meet the demands of the new 'science' of building conservation and new repair methods need to be tried, and shown to be proven over time, otherwise no alternatives will be developed. This does not justify the indiscriminate use of new techniques on older buildings, rather, a balance has to be reached, where reasoned and informed experimentation is carried out, but kept to a minimum, and proven materials are used wherever possible.

The repairs developed at the museum were based upon considerable understanding and appreciation of timber-framed buildings as well as a clear philosophical approach free of commercial pressures to devise a quick-fix marketable solution.

The repair solutions were developed in a museum environment, on buildings that were not listed or protected. This enabled a more experimental approach to be adopted than may otherwise have been acceptable. This work will prove beneficial not just to the museum but also to others involved with the repair of older buildings. Even where resins or methods similar to those adopted at the museum are not used, their success will stimulate ideas and repair solutions using traditional materials, such as the repairs to a listed building illustrated in Case Study 3.4.

Case Study 3.4 Minimising the loss of timber

Figure 3.16a

Figure 3.16b

Figure 3.16c

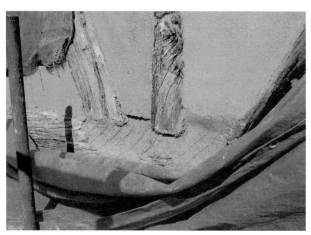

Figure 3.16d

In this case, impervious cement renders were removed (figure 3.16b) as they were providing a serious threat of decay to the structural timber-frame of a Grade II* listed building (also see Case Studies 2.3 and 3.2). The circumstances meant that traditional carpentry repairs would have resulted in the loss of a significant amount of historic fabric. To joint new timbers to the existing fabric would cause an unacceptable amount of historic timber to be lost.

The solution devised in this case was to combine concealed metal strap repairs (figure 3.16c) – to reinstate the structural performance of the decayed timbers – with the imaginative use of lime based mortar and clay tiles. This enabled the frame to be repaired using compatible materials with a minimum amount of intervention. The cement plasters were replaced with earth and lime based renders (figure 3.16d), which were applied with limewash, once

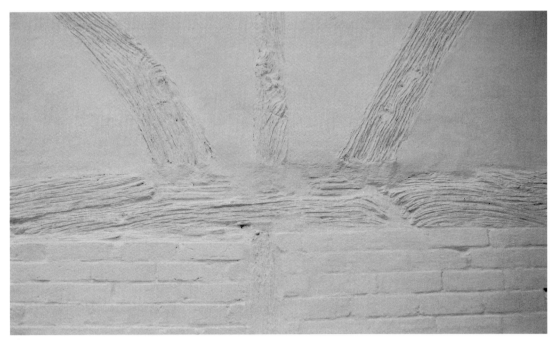

Figure 3.16e

the underlying fabric had been repaired and consolidated.

There was minimal loss of historic fabric and the work carried out is reversible. This repair was based upon reasoned decisions using materials that are proven to be compatible with the traditional performance of the building. A patchwork appearance was avoided and a unified finish provided that offers the building improved protection against the elements (figure 3.16e).

A framework for success

The highly individual nature of older buildings and the many circumstances and situations that can be encountered, prevent any guidance from being prescriptive. Nevertheless, it is critical to achieve a sound philosophical framework to work within, as this will improve the chances of advice, recommendations and specifications being appropriate and sympathetic to the building in question.

> You should…cast a questioning eye over everything you see done in the name of conservation, from the least demanding 'lick and a promise' to the most unsympathetic commercial blastaway refurbishment. Philosophical insights are to be gained from a consideration of the humdrum and the frankly awful as well as the exemplary.[17]

References

1   Earl, J., *Building Conservation Philosophy*, Third Edition, Donhead Publishing, Shaftesbury, 2003, p. 50.

2   Technical Conservation, Research and Education Division, *TAN 11 Fire Protection Measures in Scottish Historic Buildings*, Historic Scotland, Edinburgh, 1997, section 1.2.3, p. 2.

3   Easton, T., 'Ritual marks on historic timber', *The Mortice and Tenon*, No. 7, Spring 1998, pp. 6–9.

4   Smith, L., 'Compass, cut circle and daisy wheel', *The Mortice and Tenon*, No. 5, Spring 1997, pp. 3–5.

5   Smith, L., 'Evidence of geometrical building design of Ty-Mawr', *The Montgomeryshire Collections*, Vol. 89, 2001, p. 135.

6   Moir, J. and Letts, J., *Thatch: Thatching in England 1790–1940*, English Heritage Research Transactions, Vol. 5, November 1999.

7   Earl, J., *Building Conservation Philosophy*, Third Edition, Donhead Publishing, Shaftesbury, 2003, p. 145.

8   Earl, J., *Building Conservation Philosophy*, Third Edition, Donhead Publishing, Shaftesbury, 2003, p. 147.

9   William Morris, SPAB 12th Annual Report, 1889.

10 Parissien, S., *Adam Style*, Phaidon Press, London, 1992, pp. 42, 61.

11 Powys, A.R., *Repair of Ancient Buildings*, Third Edition, The Society for the Protection of Ancient Buildings, London, 1995.

12 *British Standard BS 7913: Guide to the Principles of the Conservation of Historic Buildings*, BSI, 1998, Section 5.2 Application of standards and codes of practice, p. 4.

13 Brereton, C., *The Repair of Historic Buildings: advice on principles and methods*, English Heritage, 1991, pp. 7–11.

14 Ridout, B., *Timber Decay In Buildings: the conservation approach to treatment*, English Heritage, Historic Scotland, 2000, pp. 138–9.

15 Townsend, A. *Repair of Wood Windows*, Technical Pamphlet 13, The Society for the Protection of Ancient Buildings, 1998.

16 Champion, R., and Harris, R., 'Repairing mortice faces', *The Mortice and Tenon*, No. 8, Spring 1999, p. 10.

17 Earl, J., *Building Conservation Philosophy*, Third Edition, Donhead Publishing, Shaftesbury, 2003, p. 147.

SUSTAINABILITY

4

Sustainability: development that meets the needs of the present without compromising the ability of future generations to meet their own needs.[1]

Valid concerns over the greenhouse effect, ozone depletion, the depletion of natural resources, the rapidly diminishing bio-diversity of habitats and species, and the pollution of the environment (the atmosphere/air, water and the internal environment) cannot be ignored, they have to become a priority, at the forefront of all our decisions.

The survey and repair of buildings does not have a track record of taking environmental considerations into account in the decision-making process, and although there are similarities in approach in building conservation and environmental conservation, the battles over preserving historic buildings have previously been fought largely on the grounds of architectural and historical issues, not environmental ones.

The presence of legislation that formally recognises historic buildings as having special architectural or historic interest reflects the acceptance of their importance and value to society.

> The Government has committed itself to the concept of sustainable development – of not sacrificing what future generations will value for the sake of short-term and often illusory gains...This commitment has particular relevance to the preservation of the historic environment, which by its nature is irreplaceable.[2]

Irrespective of this protection, many historic buildings continue to be put at danger from commercial pressures, the use of inappropriate materials, an emphasis on replacement rather than repair, and in the worst case demolition. These threats are increased where buildings do not have the benefit of protection by listing, such as in the recent cases of the two unlisted seventeenth-century cottages that were considered not to be of a suitable standard for listing and were demolished, but not without local resistance, only to be replaced by modern houses.[3,4]

> The immediate and obvious objective of building conservation is to secure the preservation of the nation's stock of buildings, and in particular its historic buildings and fine architecture, in the long term interest of society. The underlying objectives are cultural, economic and environmental.[5]

It is important to accentuate the positive attributes, and the significant contribution that the existing building stock can make to a sustainable future. Actively promoting the benefits of these buildings is the only way that any value will be placed on them. For example, the regular survey of the investment performance of listed office buildings shows that listed offices have consistently achieved a higher total income return than unlisted offices.[6]

One area where there is significant scope for improvement is in the sustainable management of those buildings that are of a traditional construction. If the decay suffered by these buildings continues at the current rate, or, as is more likely, accelerates, a significant amount of fabric will be irreparably lost. This will increase the demands made on finite natural resources for materials needed to repair or replace these buildings. To enable the existing building stock to be managed in a sustainable way, current attitudes need to change. This can be achieved by giving a greater emphasis to adaptation and repair rather than demolition and wholesale replacement. If tangible progress is to be made we need a fully integrated approach that includes mainstream practitioners, not just a small group of specialists working on the periphery, because we all have a responsibility to act. We cannot wait to pass this responsibility onto future generations, as this will be too little too late.

Sustainable development is a term commonly used in the construction industry, where, it can be argued, the emphasis is on financial return rather than global benefit. Although economic sustainability is a necessity, it cannot be at the cost of social, cultural and environmental values. Where financial gain is given priority in the short-term it results in solutions that are damaging, both financially and environmentally, in the longer-term. The combination of sustainability and development can lead to action that is detrimental to the existing building stock and the environment, for instance, delaying a project until it is economically viable. Such a delay can lead to accelerated deterioration and loss of fabric in a building already in a poor condition, thus imposing greater demands on finite resources when it becomes economically viable to start the project. Where there will be delay there needs to be investment in protecting the existing fabric against deterioration to reduce the demands on the resources that are needed to

Figure 4.1 This bungalow was demolished to allow the construction of two new houses. It was constructed in 1957, and was in a sound structural condition, still having a serviceable life at the time of demolition; most of the materials from the building were not re-used. The net gain was one additional house. The loss was the materials and the embodied energy of the bungalow, the drain on resources and energy embodied in the construction of two new houses. Such an approach to the existing building stock is a waste of existing resources and an example of putting commercial priorities before sustainable development.

bring the building into an economic and viable use. To achieve truly sustainable solutions requires all the criteria for sustainability to be met, not just those that are convenient or appropriate for short-term goals.

> The houses that we build and renovate today should survive us and last well into the next century, a time when our current environmental crisis will be more acute. Our building practice should alleviate as much as possible the environmental debt which the next generation is going to have to pay.[7]

ADOPTING A SUSTAINABLE APPROACH

> Green building is not simply about protecting the biosphere and natural resources from over-exploitation or over-consumption, nor is it simply about saving energy to reduce our heating bills, it considers the impact of buildings and materials on occupants and the impact of our lives on the future of the Earth.[8]

Practitioners who encounter existing buildings in their everyday work need to adopt an approach that is respectful of the past, consistent with the intended performance of the building, and sustainable for the future.

For a sustainable approach to be effective we need to preserve what we have by looking after traditional buildings in an appropriate manner. Global concerns need to be taken into account in the decision-making process; a 'greener' approach is urgently needed, one that places an onus on good stewardship, of acting as trustees for those that come after us. This approach was developed in the nineteenth century by John Ruskin and William Morris, and is just as, if not more, relevant today.

The idea of self-denial for the sake of posterity, of practising present economy for the sake of debtors yet unborn, of planting forests that our descendants may live under their shade, or of raising cities for future nations to inhabit, never, I suppose, efficiently takes place among publicly recognised motives of exertion. Yet these are not the less our duties; nor is our part fully sustained upon the earth; unless the range of our intended and deliberate usefulness include, not only the companions but the successors of our pilgrimage. God has lent us the earth for our life; it is a great entail. It belongs as much to those who are to come after us, and whose names are already written in the book of creation, as to us; and we have no right, by anything that we do or neglect, to involve them in unnecessary penalties, or deprive them of benefits which it was in our power to bequeath ... Men cannot benefit those that are with them as they can benefit those who come after them; and of all the pulpits from which the human voice is ever sent forth, there is none from which it reaches so far as from the grave.[9]

The embodied energy invested in the building fabric and the value of the cultural knowledge and information embodied within these buildings provide us with tangible links with our past. In most cases these buildings can remain highly functional and continue in beneficial use if allowed to perform as intended and are repaired and maintained in a sympathetic manner. Attitudes regarding how buildings should function are coming full-circle. Many traditional buildings are seen as excellent models for new buildings that strive to be sustainable in their design and construction. 'Breathability' is now a high profile benefit, no longer exclusive to traditional buildings, upon which many materials and systems are marketed, from vapour-permeable roofing felts to paints.

Figure 4.2 The repair, consolidation and protection of the wall heads of a standing ruin, protected as a scheduled ancient monument. The conventional method of protection for the wall head is to use a cement or hard lime flaunching. This can result in problems of performance as well as producing a sterile environment that is not necessarily aesthetically pleasing. An alternative is to use a soft capping of turf. This will provide sufficient protection whilst improving with age the appearance of the ruin. It will also provide a new habitat for wildlife and fauna. The embodied energy used is minimal and adds life and value to the structure.

ENVIRONMENTAL QUALITIES OF EXISTING BUILDINGS

Embodied energy

Embodied energy is the energy used in the construction of the building: from the extraction of raw materials, through to manufacture of components, processing and packaging, transportation, installation, and finally, demolition and disposal. In modern terms this energy is likely to be almost entirely fossil-fuel based, and therefore contributing to CO_2 emissions.

Many older buildings were constructed using traditional materials that will have been subjected to little or no processing or manufacturing. In many cases, particularly before the Industrial Revolution, it is likely that what processing did take place will have been achieved without the use of fossil fuel, but using other sources, such as timber (bio-mass). The local, vernacular, origins of most of the materials will have minimised the distance materials were transported, and many materials used in construction, and in subsequent repair and maintenance, will be close to their natural state. Consequently, the embodied energy of the fabric used to construct and repair many older buildings is very low, particularly in comparison with modern buildings.

Case Study 4.1 Low embodied energy repairs

Water used by the fire brigade to put out a thatch fire to a Grade II listed cottage caused considerable damage to wall and ceiling plaster, which was primarily earth rather than lime-based. The fire brigade managed to save a significant amount of medieval thatch, but in areas where it was damaged by fire and removed, the roof timbers were exposed. It was found that the roof frame had minimal restraint and did not meet engineering calculations.

The building was originally a medieval open-hall, with the roof containing a large quantity of smoke-blackened thatch and timbers. Alternatives to the widespread installation of large metal straps were therefore sought in planning the repair to minimise disturbance of the medieval fabric.

Riven oak battens were carefully screw-fixed to the rafters to replace missing and damaged battens, thus enabling the thatch to be secured to the roof. The battens were screw-fixed to reduce damage to surviving plaster finishes and smoke-blackened medieval timbers. A case was made that the battens were adequate enough to stiffen the roof frame to the engineer's satisfaction.

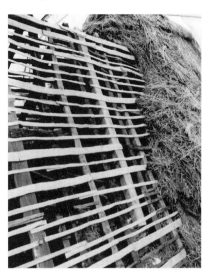

Figure 4.3 New riven oak battens provided a firm base for re-thatching and stiffened the roof frame.

Figure 4.4a Damage to ceiling plaster caused by water used to put out a fire to the thatched roof.

Figure 4.4b Earth plaster repairs. Note only damaged plaster has been replaced.

To repair the damaged plasterwork, earth was salvaged from the collapsed ceilings and was reconstituted with earth dug from the garden. This was combined with some lime mortar and reinstated. The earth for the repairs was probably dug from the same ground used for the original walls and ceilings, and it was found that there was a great consistency and compatibility in the performance between the old and new, with surprising little shrinkage in the finished plaster.

The embodied energy in this building would have been significantly increased if modern mass-produced plasters had been used, as there would have been an increase in costs relating to the extraction, production and transportation of the materials, particularly had they been imported.

This case study illustrates the simplicity and availability of materials taken for granted, that have a proven performance over centuries. The primary purpose of the riven oak battens is to enable the thatch to be secured to the roof, but they also provided structural stiffening of the roof frame thus avoiding the need for the introduction of steel straps.

Figure 4.4c The ceiling repaired. This has been achieved using materials compatible and consistent with the original.

Traditional methods of construction do not create excessive pollution and traditional materials are, in the main, relatively environmentally benign. Conversely, many modern materials have comparatively high embodied energy levels, the production processes and their components are by and large pollutants, that are potentially damaging to the health of the people who construct and occupy the buildings. For environmentalists, one of the most notorious modern materials are thermoplastics, the most common of which is PVC. Concern has been expressed for many years about the high levels of dioxins and other organochlorines found in high concentration around PVC production plants and released to the atmosphere on combustion. In chemical terms, thermoplastics are not solids but viscoelastic liquids, and like any fluid they will evaporate or off-gas, especially when subjected to light, pressure or heat. The softer thermoplastics, which contain plasticisers, tend to be less stable – with even unplasticised PVC (uPVC) containing up to 12 per cent plasticiser by weight. The highly persistent toxins associated with thermoplastics are soluble in fat rather than water, and so accumulate in the food chain and fatty tissues in the body. They have been linked with cancer, immune system damage and hormone disruption.[10]

The fact that the process of building is now categorised under the umbrella of the 'construction industry' reflects the move away from the simple ecologically sound methods of traditional construction to one more reliant upon mass-produced materials and products. The cement industry is the second largest emitter of CO_2 in the UK after the electricity generation industry. Worldwide, the cement industry has been calculated as contributing to approximately ten per cent of all CO_2 emissions.

> We have to face up to the fact that the construction industry is one of the biggest – if not the biggest – consumers of energy in our society. Materials are brought vast distances, materials are imposed with no sense of local or cultural appropriateness, and materials are used with little sense of their long-term weathering and maintenance values.[11]

The investment of embodied cultural value

The workmanship, skill and knowledge of the craftsmen who originally constructed and repaired traditional buildings needs to be included in any assessment of their value. Although difficult to quantify this is an essential part of what makes old buildings special. It is not just the economic value or the level of embodied energy incorporated in their construction that is important, but the fact that in many instances fabric lost can never be replicated in the same manner, or to the same standard. No matter how much we try, it will never be authentic.

The educational value of many older buildings is also important, particularly as the process of discovering and re-learning continues into why they were constructed, and the cultural information they contain. These buildings contain evidence of many traditional skills and techniques that no longer survive. This loss of skilled knowledge has been compounded by the demise of the apprenticeship schemes in many building firms, so the link with the past is being severed, placing a greater value on the information contained within these buildings. If we forget how to repair and maintain them, we cannot look after them.

Durable and proven

Modern buildings are built with a minimum life expectancy (usually expressed as 60 years), whereas, older buildings, by the virtue of their very existence, have a proven durability.

Many traditional buildings that survive today have only done so because they have been adapted and changed over time to meet the demands and requirements of subsequent owners and users. This flexibility has allowed these buildings to continue in use without creating the demand for much further investment in materials. These qualities are the very virtues of sustainability.

Ease of maintenance and repair

The measuring of likely repairs and maintenance throughout the lifetime of a building is termed life analysis. This is commonly arrived at on either an energy or cost basis. The common perception is that older buildings require high levels of maintenance, but as with modern buildings, the levels of maintenance needed are dependent upon the size and type of building, materials and detailing, the exposure of the building to the elements and how often routine maintenance, such as clearing of gutters, is carried out.

Firstly, we need to compare like with like. As modern buildings age, many of the materials used in construction will be shown not to be as durable or as adaptable as those used on older buildings. In many instances modern timber replacement windows or timber repairs will have failed within a short space of time, as a result of poor selection, poor quality of timber and poor detailing. It is not uncommon to find that the original Georgian sash window has outlasted repairs carried out within the last 20 years. Traditionally constructed buildings can be easily repaired and maintained, for example, a badly spalled brick can be readily replaced with a new brick. Similarly, the 'softness' of traditional lime or earth mortar allows piecemeal repair, whereas bricks bedded in cement mortar would be incapable of being easily replaced or reused in the future. The use of materials that are readily available and can be easily replaced when they are at the end of their useful life is one of the key factors in the longevity of many older buildings. Lime mortar also has the advantage of allowing bricks or stone to be reused in the future, whereas the use of cement would preclude the recycling of materials.

Many modern materials and solutions provide only short-term gains, or cosmetically conceal problems. They often treat only the symptoms, and not the causes, and in some cases will actually prejudice future repairs and the ability to reuse and salvage existing fabric.

> **Insulating foam** Isocyanurate is sometimes sprayed directly onto the underside of slates and tiles, and sets into a hard layer with strong adhesive properties. Foams are claimed to improve insulation and waterproofing, prevent tiles or slates slipping, and avoid condensation. **Sprayed insulated foams on slates and tiles are NOT recommended for historic buildings:** they prevent the slates and tiles being salvaged during the next re-roofing, the tiling battens and the upper parts of the rafters are sealed in, which may lead to rotting and premature degradation, and the normal flow of air into the roof space is restricted.[12]

Modern buildings are constructed principally with mass-produced products or specifically designed finishes, components and systems; the life of the building is dictated by the availability of these components. When materials, or one-offs, are no longer produced the building cannot be easily maintained or repaired and the cost, both financially and physically, therefore increases significantly. Eventually the building will become uneconomic to maintain. The functionality of the building may therefore outlive the serviceable life of the materials, which can become obsolescent very early in the life of a modern building. A 'cradle to grave' approach to the design of modern buildings and the repair and maintenance of existing buildings needs to be adopted to overcome the poor management and waste of resources.

In traditional buildings, even materials that have a short-life or require high levels of maintenance, can usually be easily replaced and have a minimal environmental impact. For example, thatch requires regular work to the ridge (on average every 10–15 years) and to the slopes (on average between 15–50 years). The life of thatch is dependent on type and quality of materials, quality of workmanship, and the degree of exposure to the elements. Despite its relatively short life and high maintenance requirements, thatch is a renewable material with very low embodied energy. The principal energy cost will be in the transportation of materials, particularly where imported thatch is used; indicating that efforts to grow indigenous crops for thatching should be encouraged.

The move away from traditional materials and methods of construction has resulted in increased importation of building products, leading to increased transportation costs, and cost of embodied energy. This is not sustainable.

To achieve a truly sustainable approach, the life costs and energy in the manufacture, use, repair, maintenance, demolition and disposal of the building and its fabric, all need to be assessed and evaluated. Making a decision based on one criterion to the exclusion of another will inevitably have a detrimental influence on the building, and therefore have a negative impact on the environment, either directly or indirectly. The embodied energy of a building and the impact it has on the environment during its life is as important as determining the energy performance in use. A holistic approach is required that is based upon an understanding of the building in question and the overall aims of sustainability.

The embodied energy of an older building will be low, however its performance in use is high – hence the need to improve the energy efficiency of the existing building stock. The energy used to run a modern, energy-efficient building can exceed the energy used in construction some six years after it was built, just one-tenth of the way into its projected 60-year life. When viewed from this perspective the embodied energy of any building is of little consequence in comparison with the energy consumed in use.

Nevertheless the manner in which energy efficiency is achieved does not always provide long-term solutions. The use of products, such as uPVC windows, with high embodied energy, do not stand up well to life cost analysis, particularly when fabric that still has a serviceable life is replaced. Such an approach to the problems we face is not truly sustainable, it will help in achieving arbitrary targets but will result in the depletion of existing fabric and finite natural resources whilst contributing to pollution and potential health problems.

NEW CHALLENGES

Energy efficiency

It is important to appreciate that although most modern buildings are designed and constructed to be energy efficient in use, they do make considerable demands on what are finite resources. They are also heavily dependent on sources of fossil fuels, which contribute to pollution. Older buildings are not as energy efficient in use as new buildings but their demands on existing resources are considerably less, particularly where they are repaired and maintained in an appropriate manner on a regular basis.

The energy performance of the existing historic building stock has been targeted for improvement, with justification, because in comparison with new buildings they are not thermally efficient in use. Greenhouse gas emissions must be reduced to have any impact on slowing global warming; one of the principal ways that this can be achieved is by reducing fossil fuel use and consequent CO_2 emissions.

There are potential dangers where the energy efficiency of existing buildings is assessed without taking into account the impact of solutions promoted as being able to reduce fuel consumption. Measures that concentrate solely on reducing fossil fuel consumption can do so to the exclusion of other important factors; where this is the case they will inevitably not be beneficial to the building, its occupants, or the environment. For example, reducing draughts by the installation of draught excluders or double-glazing, can reduce the ability of moisture in the building fabric to evaporate and create an internal environment conducive to mould growth and dust mites. These dangers arise, as do many others, where a holistic approach to problems is not adopted.

Meeting new expected standards of performance by adapting the existing building stock will be a new challenge.

> In environmental terms, the continued use of existing building stock, whether or not of particular architectural merit or historic interest, coupled with measures to improve energy efficiency, is a global priority. New build construction, by comparison, is a major user of non-renewable resources and energy.
>
> The relative cheapness of new construction, as an alternative to the re-use of existing buildings, is often derived from scale, mechanization of the process and from the relatively low cost of labour and resources needed. While the conservation and continued use of existing buildings can depend disproportionately on the use of skilled craftsmen and traditional building methods.
>
> Existing buildings, by comparison, contain embodied energy, derived largely from the labour invested in them when they were built, which is dissipated and lost when they are destroyed. The materials and traditional building methods used in conservation, although demanding of labour and skill, are, nevertheless, economical in terms of non-renewable energy resources. They are also inherently maintainable and almost benign in terms of toxicity.
>
> However, improvements to the thermal insulation properties of existing buildings, to enable them to match the low levels of energy use achieved in many new buildings, can often be difficult to achieve. In the case of architecturally or historically important buildings, such improvements can often be impossible without alterations that can be unacceptably damaging in other ways. Nevertheless, in global environmental terms, the balance of advantage strongly favours the retention of existing building stock, particularly where performance in terms of energy consumption in use can be improved.[13]

The use of the term 'embodied energy' has to be used carefully in the context of existing buildings, as it is commonly used to describe the total amount of energy used in the construction of a new building. It should not be confused with the embodied cultural value that reflects the craftsmanship and aesthetic values of the building that is not as easily definable.

The practitioner must be alert to the dangers posed to traditional buildings when being adapted to meet new and improved standards of performance. Fabric can be put at risk from replacement, alteration and adaptation or decay, particularly where standard solutions are adopted to improve thermal performance.

The 2002 edition of Building Regulations Approved Document Part L seeks to improve the energy performance of all buildings, including existing ones, when altered, extended or subjected to change of use. The importance of the performance of historic buildings, and the appreciation that their special interest could be compromised in trying to comply with the Regulations, are recognised in the new document.

The recognition offered by the Building Regulations is important, as it acknowledges that a building's traditional 'breathing' performance needs to be taken into consideration before making any alterations and that irreparable damage can be caused by trying to meet new standards in inappropriate ways.

The Building Regulations' definition of what constitutes a historic building is based upon those buildings that are formally recognised in one form or another and includes:

- listed buildings
- buildings which are situated in conservation areas
- buildings of local architectural or historical interest and which are referred to as a material consideration in a local authority's development plan
- buildings of architectural and historical interest within national parks, areas of outstanding natural beauty, and world heritage sites[14]

Since approximately 25 per cent of the existing building stock is of a traditional construction, with only three per cent falling into the Building Regulations definition of historic, the separation of buildings of a traditional construction that are protected, from those that are not, disregards the needs and requirements of 22 per cent of the existing building stock. The breathing performance is just as relevant to the condition and longevity of those traditional buildings that fall outside the Building Regulations classification of 'historic'. The recognition by the Building Regulations that there is a need to '...[make] provisions enabling the fabric [of historic buildings] to 'breathe' to control moisture and potential long term decay problems' is evidence of this.[15]

The omission of specific reference in the Building Regulations to those buildings that fall outside the 'historic' classification, but are nevertheless of a traditional construction, means that they will be at increased risk of exposure to inappropriate modifications in order to make reasonable provision for the conservation of fuel and power. This is in addition to requirements for work to comply with regulations relating to structural safety, fire safety and access for disabled people.

It could be argued that all buildings of a traditional construction should be treated in a manner that reflects their individual performance characteristics and needs. This would minimise the introduction of changes or improvements that may be detrimental to a building's performance and condition. This can be achieved in many cases by making improvements in the thermal performance of other elements of the building.[16]

One method of determining the thermal performance of a building is via an energy rating report, such as a SAP (Standard Assessment Procedure). The Building Regulations ensure that energy rating reports will play an increasingly important role in the assessment of the condition and performance of buildings. There are however hidden dangers in using a standard assessment for examining traditional buildings, as they can be highly individual. Energy ratings can result in standard recommendations being made to improve thermal efficiency – such as installing efficient heating systems, the provision of insulation, draught exclusion and double-glazing. The arbitrary way that these standard measures can be applied may have a detrimental impact upon the buildings of a traditional construction, resulting from the installation of inappropriately detailed insulation, and the unnecessary loss of fabric – windows being particularly vulnerable to replacement – which will influence the performance of the building.[17] Case Study 4.2 illustrates that it is not always correct to assume that significant improvements in performance can be achieved by upgrading the windows.

Timber windows with minor areas of decay or flaking paint may be perceived as being beyond economical repair, as carrying out regular routine maintenance and repair is no longer desirable. An additional problem is therefore created, because reliance on replacement rather than repair reduces the demand for those with the skills who can carry out repairs. Rather than having a standard measure that results in the replacement of windows, other solutions need to be considered, such as repair, draught-proofing and secondary glazing.

In addition to having an adverse effect on the character of the building and its locality, wholesale replacement will invariably result in the loss of serviceable fabric. Additional pressures to replace windows come via

Figure 4.5 (left)
A historic shop front. This window is not energy-efficient but is still functional and informs us of a past use now long gone. Simple measures could improve the energy efficiency of the building without the loss of irreplaceable fabric.

Figure 4.6 (right)
A more conventional approach was taken in this case, however. The historic shop window was replaced with an 'off-the shelf' double-glazed unit. Once the blockwork is rendered there will be little remaining evidence that this building was once a shop.

companies actively marketing and promoting their products; this is especially true in the case of modified unplasticised polyvinyl chloride (uPVC) double glazed windows where claims are made that they are low maintenance. However, uPVC windows will have a relatively short life span as they are vulnerable to ultraviolet degradation and cannot be repaired. Whereas timber windows, in comparison, can have their life extended by simple maintenance and repair.

A closer examination of many of the replacement options, particularly uPVC, shows that they cannot be repaired or maintained; that they are high in embodied energy; have an unknown longevity (especially with increases in ultraviolet light levels); are made from relatively complicated and highly manufactured materials; and result in pollution during their manufacture, their life, and disposal. As a result, in some countries such as Sweden, Germany and Austria, they are either banned, or there are restrictions on the use of PVC, on environmental grounds.

PVC Window Paint

A major paint company has recently developed a uPVC window paint, recommended for use every six years. This is surprising considering that one of the major selling points of uPVC window frames is their durability and low maintenance. One can only conclude that unless the company is marketing a product for which there is no practical use, then uPVC windows require a similar maintenance programme to their wooden counterparts. Painting will also increase the negative environmental impact of uPVC windows over their life span.[18]

Replacement often results in the total loss of existing fabric that still has a serviceable life. The windows, which are the eyes and soul of many older buildings, provide important information about a building's status, are an invaluable indicator of the age of a building, and are one of the principal aesthetic features. Comparison of cost in use between existing and replacement windows illustrates that rehabilitation and regular maintenance are more cost-effective in the long-run than wholesale replacement.[19]

Replacing still-serviceable fabric with materials that, at best, have dubious environmental credentials is not sustainable behaviour. If replacement is justified, then careful selection of materials is essential, to ensure that their serviceable life will be as long as the fabric that they replaced. In some cases this can be two to three-hundred years, a period significantly greater than that of a 25-year guarantee, or the limited life of a sealant. The replacement materials should ideally provide improvement in performance, and have a minimal impact on the environment.

Every effort needs to be made for serviceable fabric to be retained, on the grounds of being cost effective and more environmentally efficient in the longer-term. Simple measures such as repairing and upgrading existing fabric can produce results to match those of modern replacements, whereas the latter may be incompatible with the building's performance and also damaging to the environment.

Figure 4.7 A pair of semi-detached cottages. The cottage on the left has been modernised, reflected in the replacement windows and the repointing with cement mortar. The cottage on the right remains unmodernised and has been neglected in recent years. Although the windows of the unmodernised cottage require some repair they are still serviceable and every effort should be made for them to be retained. Note how the replacement of the windows and the repointing in cement has changed the appearance of the modernised cottage.

Case Study 4.2 Improving performance

This case concerns a Grade II listed thatched timber-framed cottage with an efficient heating system: a condensing boiler to wall mounted radiators.

Air infiltration tests were used to assess the existing and predicted performance of the building. It was found that the building was suffering from high levels of air infiltration; i.e. it was very draughty.

The pressure test showed that the building was subject to 24 air changes per hour when subject to the 50Pa pressure. This is very draughty and far in excess of the ventilation necessary to safeguard against moisture build-up. This level of ventilation simply adds to the draughts and poor thermal comfort, leading to higher fuel bills and extra carbon dioxide pollution from increased fossil fuel use.

Figure 4.8a The thatched cottage before repair.

Figure 4.8b Note the fan equipment in the door used to assess the air infiltration at the building.

The tests revealed that draught-proofing the windows and doors would not provide significant benefits, which is not what is usually expected in an old building. In fact it was the lightweight cladding to the timber frame (the render and weatherboarding), the tiled slopes below the rear dormer windows, and gaps around the thatch that were allowing excessive amounts of air infiltration. Basic efforts had been made to insulate the walls behind weatherboarding, but no action had been taken to remove excessive draughts and the insulation was therefore ineffective (figure 4.9a).

Had the building not been listed there would have been pressure to install doubling glazing, and whilst it would have had some benefit, it would not have addressed other principal sources of draught infiltration. (Even where a building is listed there can still be pressure to replace windows.)

The solutions devised included:

1. The removal of the weatherboarding, providing naturally hygroscopic insulation (sheep's wool) to the voids between the timber frame, adding an external cladding of tongue and grooved woodfibre board to the outer side, and then replacing the weatherboarding. This added insulation and, importantly, improved draught proofing.
2. The removal of impervious cement rendering and taking the opportunity to provide naturally hygroscopic insulation (sheep's wool) to the voids between the timber frame. A lime-based render was reapplied.
3. Areas of tiling to the rear roof were re-laid with a tongue and groove woodfibre sarking board.
4. The repair of many small holes in the thatch and historic render.
5. Draught-proofing, rather than replacement, of existing windows.

Modern materials were used in the repair of the building. These are vapour permeable and were selected carefully for their environmental attributes, and to ensure that they were compatible with the building's performance.

A specialist engineer made calculations to check that the proposed detailing would not cause

interstitial condensation during normal use and that any collected moisture would be allowed to pass through the structure in the manner of traditional construction. To ensure that the intended breathing performance would not be adversely affected, air infiltration tests were carried out during the process of installation to ensure that the building was not made too airtight.

It was calculated that air changes could be reduced from the existing 24 air changes per hour, to 16 air changes per hour. This is sufficiently above the Building Research Establishment recommended target of 3–5 air changes per hour in a modern 'dry' building, but importantly allows the building to perform as intended whilst achieving tangible benefits.

Calculations showed that the repairs and alterations specified would increase the SAP rating from 49 (including the condensing heating system) to 81, reduce the CO_2 emissions from 11.1 to 5.3 tonnes per annum, and reduce the gas cost from £1076 to £536 per annum (at 2002 prices).

Figure 4.9a (top left) Gaps between the insulation and the studwork made previous attempts of insulating the building ineffective. Improved detailing is needed to make the insulation effective.

Figure 4.9b (top right) Sheep's wool insulation was provided between the studs. The external face is provided with tongue and grove woodfibre board before being re-clad with weatherboarding. Note how the joints and junctions are provided with additional protection against draughts.

Figure 4.9c (bottom left) The weatherboarding being applied over the woodfibre board.

Figure 4.9d (bottom centre) The removal of cement render to the front elevation allowed sheep's wool insulation to be provided between the exposed timber frame.

Figure 4.9e (bottom right) A lime putty render made to match surviving historic finishes replaces the cement render.

The fabric was repaired using materials and methods compatible with its intended performance, and the air tightness of the building was also improved. By taking a holistic approach the negative impact of the building on the environment is reduced. The air infiltration tests identified the actual problems being suffered and thereby assisted in the devising of a bespoke solution, that allowed resources to be targeted at eliminating actual, rather than perceived, draughts.

The resultant increase in comfort levels and the reduction of fuel consumption will make the building a more attractive place to live, and will extend the building's beneficial life. CO_2 emissions are reduced and a positive contribution to reducing greenhouse gases and the environment is made. This case study illustrates that given the right circumstances, and great care, improvements can be made to older buildings that do not detract from either their appearance or their performance.

Measures to improve the energy efficiency of a building, or increases in the standard of comfort, can create pressures for improvements in the building services such as the introduction of heating systems. Where alterations are proposed great care will be needed as changes or the provision of services can cause considerable physical damage and also change the performance of buildings, which can result in the damage of historic fabric.[20,21]

Responding to environmental changes

Our changing environment is creating new challenges for those who are responsible for the preservation of older buildings. Changes in the intensity of prevailing winds, increased levels of rainfall, and resultant flooding, and extremes in ground conditions will all lead to existing philosophy and practices being questioned.

Measures not usually associated with the repair of traditional buildings may have to be taken into consideration where environmental conditions have dramatically changed and are putting condition and functionality at risk. For some buildings this may mean that their appearance has to be changed so that they are able to combat the new environmental conditions. Advocating this, particularly for buildings that are listed or situated in conservation areas, will meet with resistance, and raises the question: Should practicality take precedent over appearance?

Where alterations are justified as being necessary to the long-term well-being of the building, where they will cause minimal intervention, and are reversible, then a strong case for making the alterations can be made. A practical response to what are likely to be increasing problems may be required to ensure that the building can continue in beneficial use. There is also a strong argument for allowing the building to be adapted if the action will allow a building to be brought back into use.

Case Study 4.3 Addressing the causes of damp

Figure 4.10 A passing heavy goods vehicle dwarfs the small cottage to the left of the terrace. The spray from passing traffic is one of the chief causes of damp in the building.

A small unlisted nineteenth-century cottage that is not located in a conservation area constructed in nine-inch solid brick walls with very porous bricks. The cottage fronts directly onto a busy A road. It is usually tenanted, but it is not occupied as it suffers from problems of damp.

The primary causes of dampness are identified as:

1. The elevation fronting onto the road is south-west facing and will be particularly exposed to driving rain.
2. The cottage suffers from spray and splashing from passing vehicles in wet weather – particularly HGVs that dwarf the building.

The two principal causes of dampness to the building – the influence of the prevailing elements and the main road – cannot be removed. To provide any effective preventative measures a drastic change in the building's appearance is required. Physically cladding the exterior of the building is the only means of providing a protective barrier against these significant causes of dampness. In the circumstances the most appropriate type of cladding would be tile hanging. Tile hanging, particularly mathematical tiles, would be aesthetically acceptable and would also be more resilient to continued splashing and spraying than a render, which would discolour and break down due to the high level of road salts present. Tile hanging

would also enable the wall behind to be ventilated, which would aid the drying out of the walls.

If predicted changes in environmental conditions are correct, with increases in rainfall and road traffic, then this building will be subjected to increased levels of dampness. External tile cladding would provide an effective means of defence for the building.

Figures 4.11a and 4.11b A cottage situated in an exposed location that suffered from penetrating dampness from driving rain. Before repair the south west facing elevation had already been partly tile hung, this provided a precedent for an appropriate solution to the problem of penetrating damp. To remove the principal cause of damp it was recommended that the whole elevation be tile hung. Listed building consent was granted and, as can be seen in figure 4.14b, the building clad and provided with improved protection from the elements.

USE OF MODERN MATERIALS

We no longer have access to the full palette of materials, or the necessary knowledge and skills, that were available when many traditional buildings were being constructed – even as late as the Victorian or Edwardian period. So it is inevitable that modern materials will need to be used to repair or to make alterations to traditional buildings.

If traditional materials are not available, and new materials need to be used, it is important that they are subjected to careful selection and specification. The materials for the repair of traditional buildings firstly need to be:

1. proven in their durability
2. readily available – to enable future maintenance and repair
3. compatible with existing fabric

The selection and specification of modern materials should have the environment in mind. The materials need to:

1. from renewable sustainable sources
2. have low embodied energy
3. be free of ozone damaging gases
4. be of minimal risk to health through out its life cycle[22]

Material	From renewable sustainable sources	Low embodied energy	Free of ozone damaging gases	Minimal risk to health throughout its life cycle
Thatch (traditional)	■	■	■	■
Reed board (modern)	■	■	■	■
Timber (traditional and modern – if from sustainable sources)	■	■	■	■
Sheep's wool (modern)	■	■	■	■
Limewash (traditional)	–	–	■	■
Earth plaster (traditional and modern)	–	■	■	■
Casein paint (traditional and modern)	–	■	■	■
Woodfibre board (modern)	■	■	■	■
PVC (modern)	–	–	–	–

Table 4.1 Basic assessment of environmental credentials of a selection of modern and traditional materials.

As a general rule materials and techniques designed for new construction should be treated with caution and if possible avoided, as their long term or side effects on a building and its occupants are not fully understood. That said, some synthetic or natural materials used thoughtfully and skilfully, e.g. for permeable insulation, can facilitate the most conservative and economical work.[23]

It is important to avoid a standardised approach to the specification of materials, and to approach their classification with care and attention to individual characteristics. For example, there are many species of softwood timber, each having varying qualities of durability and resistance to treatment with chemical preservatives. A generic specification that softwood should be used for timber repairs can therefore mislead, as the term does not reflect the many varieties available. Great care is needed to ensure that the correct species of softwood is specified for each intended purpose, taking account of the proposed environment and the potential exposure to decay mechanisms. A considered approach to specification could prevent a lot of unnecessary treatment of timber.[24]

Even the simple insertion of insulation into a building needs to be given careful thought, to determine whether the performance characteristics of the materials available are compatible with the performance of the building.

Sheep's wool is derived from renewable resources and has relatively low embodied energy. It therefore has environmental benefits over many other conventional alternatives. These factors, together with life cost analysis, should be important considerations when assessing what materials to use in the repair and improvement of the existing building stock.

	Fibreglass insulation	Sheep's wool insulation
Positive attributes	▪ Cost ▪ Availability	▪ Minimal resource depletion ▪ Low embodied energy ▪ Breathable/hygroscopic ▪ Retains thermal performance when damp ▪ No health risk ▪ Bio-degradable
Negative attributes	▪ Resource depletion ▪ High-embodied energy ▪ Retains moisture ▪ Potential health risks, contains toxins ▪ Not user friendly – can cause irritation ▪ Poor thermal performance when damp ▪ Increased risk of mould and fungal growth ▪ Disposal, non-bio-degradable ▪ Acid rain – emissions of oxides linked with glass production	▪ Resins used to stabilise some products–increasing the embodied energy and production costs ▪ Financially expensive in comparison ▪ Need to cut and dress when installing ▪ Most wool is imported and this increases the embodied energy costs

Table 4.2 Comparison between sheep's wool and fibreglass insulation.

PRINCIPLES OF GREEN BUILDING

The following examples of green building measures are reproduced from the *Green Building Handbook (Volume 1)* that acknowledges 'that the building materials industry, the transportation of materials and products, their construction on site and then the pollution and energy wastage coming from buildings collectively has a surprising wider impact on the environment than most other human activities'.[25]

The four principal aims (a) – (d) provide a sound template from which a sustainable holistic approach can be devised for each building encountered. I see no direct conflict between the green building approach and that of building conservation as there are many parallels, with the

a. Reducing energy in use	b. Minimising external pollution and environmental damage
for example	*for example*
▪ Use maximum possible low embodied energy insulation, but with good ventilation ▪ Use low energy lighting and electrical appliances ▪ Use efficient, low polluting heating ▪ Make use of passive and active solar energy wherever feasible ▪ Use passive and natural ventilation systems rather than mechanical	▪ Design in harmonious relationship with the surroundings ▪ Avoid destruction of natural habitats ▪ Re-use rainwater on site (particularly where mains drainage is not available) ▪ Treat and recycle waste water on site if possible (particularly where mains drainage is not available) ▪ Try to minimise extraction of minerals unless good environmental controls exist and avoid materials which produce damaging chemicals as a by product ▪ Do not dump waste materials off site but re-use on site
c. Reducing embodied energy and resource depletion	d. Minimising internal pollution and damage to health
for example	*for example*
▪ Use locally sourced materials ▪ Use materials found on site ▪ Minimise use of imported materials ▪ Use materials from sustainably managed sources ▪ Keep use of materials from non-renewable sources to a minimum ▪ Use low energy materials, keeping high embodied energy materials to a minimum ▪ Use secondhand or recycled materials where appropriate ▪ Re-use existing buildings and structures instead of always assuming that new buildings are required	▪ Use non toxic material, or low emission materials ▪ Avoid fibres from insulation materials getting into the atmosphere ▪ Ensure good natural ventilation ▪ Reduce dust and allergens ▪ Reduce impact of electromagnetic fields (EMFs) ▪ Create positive character in the building and relationship with site ▪ Involve users in design and management of building and evaluating environmental choices

Table 4.3 Principles of green building.

exception of the use of second-hand/recycled materials, that can lead to the stripping of viable buildings. Nevertheless, practitioners face many challenges before a sustainable 'cradle to the grave' approach is achieved. For instance they will need all their skills to reconcile the potential conflict and differences that exist between doing as little as possible to an existing building whilst being seen to be making a positive contribution to the environmental concerns of today. For example, the easy option in repairing wall plaster in an older building is to use modern materials, such as cement-based plasters that may not be appropriate for the building in question. By avoiding cement and using an earth-based plaster, not only is the plaster compatible with the performance of the building, but also a more environmentally-friendly product. Although it is not from sustainable sources it has low embodied energy, as it is near its natural state and has been subject to a minimum amount of processing. It is also free of ozone-depleting gases and does not have any health implications for those who extract the material, use it in the repair of the building or for its occupants. If more people selected the materials of repair and maintenance more carefully, the impact on the environment would be significantly reduced.

> ...the National Trust has learned that conservation practices are not automatically environmentally-sustainable: conservationists must work to a code of environmental practices, which enable both the cultural and natural environment to co-exist, resist degradation and/or adapt to change.[26]

References

1 *The Brundtland Report*, United Nations World Commission on Environmental and Development, 1987.

2 Department of the Environment/Department of National Heritage, *Planning Policy Guidance Note 15, Planning and the Historic Environment*, HMSO, London, 1994, section 1.3, p.1. At the time of writing PPG15 is under review.

3 Stummer, R., 'Born circa 1602: lawfully demolished in July – so where was the protection?, *SPAB News*, Vol. 23, No. 4, 2002, p. 7.

4 Stummer, R., 'Another village loses a beloved old building 'not of a standard to save', *SPAB News*, Vol. 24, No. 1, 2003, pp. 10–11.

5 *British Standard BS 7913: Guide to the Principles of the Conservation of Historic Buildings*, BSI, 1998, Section 1.1, General, p. 1.

6 The Investment Performance of Listed Buildings. RICS Foundation, London, 2002.

7 Borer, P. and Harris, C., *The Whole House Book: Ecological building design and materials*, The Centre for Alternative Technology Publications, 1998, p. 6.

8 Woolley, T., Kimmins, S., Harrison, P & Harrison, R., *Green Building Handbook, Volume 1: A guide to building products and their impact on the environment*, Spon Press, London, 2001, p. 5.

9 Ruskin, J., 'The lamp of memory', *The Seven Lamps of Architecture*, 1849.

10 Borer, P. and Harris, C. *The Whole House Book: Ecological building design and materials*, The Centre for Alternative Technology Publications, 1998, pp. 126–7.

11 Burman, P., 'The ethics of using traditional building materials', in Maxwell, I. and Ross, I. (eds), *Conference Proceedings*, Historic Scotland Traditional Building Materials Conference, Crown copyright, Edinburgh, 1997.

12 *Building Regulations and Historic Buildings: Balancing the needs for energy conservation with those of building conservation– an interim guidance note on the application of Part L*, English Heritage, September 2002, p.19.

13 *British Standard BS 7913: Guide to the Principles of the Conservation of Historic Buildings*, BSI, 1998, Section 6.4.2 The global component, p. 7.

14 *The Building Regulations 2000, Approved Document L1, Conservation of fuel and power in dwellings*, 2002 edition, Paragraph 2.9 of Part L1; and *The Building Regulations 2000, Approved Document L2, Conservation of fuel and power in buildings other than dwellings*, 2002 edition, Paragraph 4.10 of Part L2, Department of Transport, Local Government and the Regions, London.

15 Ibid.

16 Innerdale, J., 'Old buildings, new rules', *SPAB News*, Vol. 23, No. 3, 2002. pp. 52–3.

17 Oxley, R., 'Further thoughts on the Building Regulations (The implications of the Standard Assessment Procedure for the future of historic buildings)', *Context*, No. 47, September 1995. pp. 15–16.

18 Woolley, T., Kimmins, S., Harrison, P and Harrison, R., *Green Building Handbook, Volume 1. A guide to building products and their impact on the environment*, Spon Press, London 2001, p. 123.

19 *Framing Opinions*, English Heritage, 1994.

20 Bordass, W., & Bemrose, C., *Heating Your Church*, Council for the Care of Churches, Church House Publishing, London, 1996.

21 *Guide To Building Services For Historic Buildings*, CIBSE, London, 2002.

22 Curwell, S., Fox, B., Greenberg, M., and March, C., *Hazardous Building Materials: A guide to the selection of environmentally responsible alternatives*, Second Edition, Spon Press, London, 2002.

23 *Building Regulations and Historic Buildings: Balancing the needs for energy conservation with those of building conservation – an interim guidance note on the application of Part L*, English Heritage, 2002, 4.8 Introducing modern materials, p. 7.

24 Scott, Cameron, 'Green wood not working', *The Mortice & Tenon*, No. 13, July 2002.

25 Woolley, T., Kimmins, S., Harrison, P & Harrison, R., *Green Building Handbook, Volume 1: A guide to building products and their impact on the environment*, Spon Press, London, 2001, pp. 6–7.

26 Jarman, R. (National Trust Environmental Practices Adviser), 'National Trust Building Projects – An Environmental Brief', *Discussion paper* for The Sustaining our Heritage Conference, jointly hosted by RICS (Royal Institute of Chartered Surveyors) & AECB (Association for Environment Conscious Building), 6 May 1999.

THE TRADITIONAL PERFORMANCE

5

...older buildings will function well if they are allowed to work as they were intended.[1]

DISTINGUISHING BETWEEN TRADITIONAL AND MODERN

The performance characteristics between traditional and modern buildings are significantly different; in most cases it will be found that modern materials and methods of repair are incompatible with buildings of a traditional construction, as they cause or exacerbate problems of dampness and decay of the fabric. The intended performance of a building dictates the appropriateness, compatibility and nature of all repairs and alterations, including those already carried out and those that will be made in the future.

In a modern building the damage or failure of one its moisture barriers will lead to severe problems of damp penetration. In an old building prevention of the evaporation of moisture from walls will lead to similar difficulties. Hence the two building types need to be handled in completely different ways: modern buildings will be damp without a barrier to moisture because the economy of design does not provide a massive and absorbent structure but old buildings will become damp if an impervious layer is applied to them because this prevents water within the structure from evaporating. As the moisture content of the wall increases, the likelihood of decay also increases.[2]

The materials and methods of construction, and of subsequent repair and maintenance, have a direct bearing on the performance and the condition of a building. An appreciation of this relationship is therefore an elementary requirement of any surveys of traditionally constructed buildings. A traditional building, its solid walls and its roof, need to 'breathe' whether it is listed or not.

> 'Breathability' (high porosity, high permeability). This group of characteristics also allows lime mortars to protect the other materials in a building by handling moisture movements through the building, protecting masonry materials from harmful salts. 'Breathability' greatly assists the drying out of buildings and the avoidance of condensation problems, which contributes to the comfort of people using the buildings.[3]

Most buildings constructed before the mid-nineteenth century were built with solid walls with no damp-proof course. With the exception of historic timber-framed structures, the walls of many traditional buildings are relatively thick, particularly in comparison with modern buildings built with thin cavity walls or lightweight timber frames.

The materials of construction were mainly porous, such as stone, brick, timber and earth. These were bedded using lime or earth based mortars and in many cases finished with lime or earth based external renders, with many traditional buildings being provided with protective limewash, that also served a decorative function. The external renders and limewash would have acted as a 'buffer' against the elements, by providing a physical but porous obstacle to extensive water absorption by the wall fabric itself. The render and limewash absorbs the rain until the conditions suitable for evaporation to take place are present.

> Protection: In many ways soft lime mortars and paints (limewash) can be used to give protection to buildings, particularly from severe rain. They can act sacrificially to protect the structure.[4]

Traditionally, pointing and many renders had an open-textured finish, for example a 'harling' or roughcast render finish. The textured finish maximises the surface area of the pointing or render and therefore increases the potential for moisture to readily evaporate from the wall.

The performance of the building can be summarised as follows:

1. Moisture is allowed to enter the porous fabric – from rain and from the ground. Damp will affect the base of the walls and the ground floor.
2. The use of traditional porous materials in the construction, and subsequent repair and maintenance, allows moisture that enters the fabric to evaporate when the atmospheric conditions are favourable, such as on sunny and/or windy days.

3. Good ventilation through the roof coverings, poorly fitting windows and openings assists evaporation of moisture.
4. Fires in regular use draw ventilation through the building and provide background radiant heat.
5. A simple lifestyle produces small amounts of water vapour.
6. The levels of dampness in the building are 'controlled' by the ability of moisture to readily evaporate.

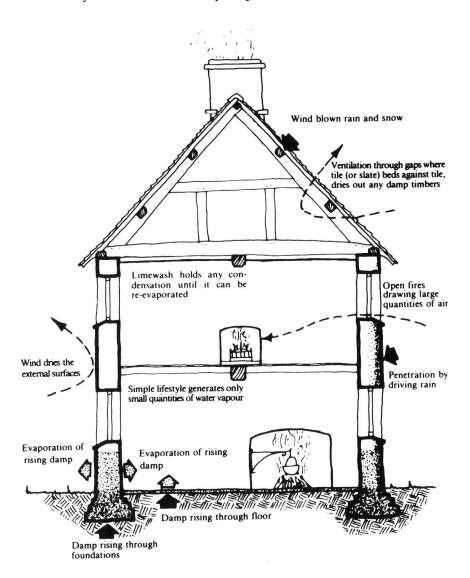

Figure 5.1 The control of damp in old buildings.[5] (Kind permission of the Society for the Protection of Ancient Buildings)

CHANGES IN THE TRADITIONAL PERFORMANCE

It is important to realise that very few older buildings of a traditional construction have escaped intervention from modern materials and methods of repair. Changes will have affected the performance and condition of these buildings and the practitioner will need to be aware of the consequences of any changes in the intended performance.

As can be seen from figures 5.1 and 5.2, changes in the way the building is used and repaired, and the introduction of impervious incompatible materials, have had a detrimental influence on the traditional breathing performance and the condition of the building:

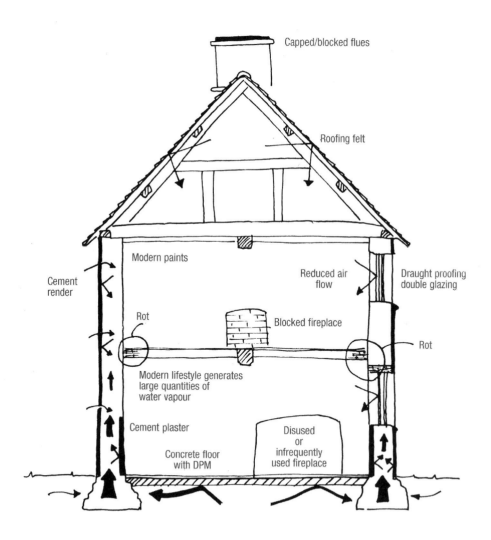

Figure 5.2 This diagram represents the same building illustrated in figure 5.1, but as it stands today having been subject to modernisation and repair with modern materials.

1. The use of impervious finishes (cement based renders, plasters and pointing and/or masonry paints) have changed it from being a 'breathable' building to one that is attempting to exclude moisture from entering the building fabric.

2. The ready evaporation of moisture that enters the walls has been significantly reduced by the introduction of impervious materials.

3. Impervious materials are generally hard and inflexible and are therefore prone to cracking. Any moisture drawn through even the finest of cracks will become entrapped behind these hard impermeable modern finishes.

4. The insertion of roofing felt reduces ventilation within the roof void.[6]

5. The provision of double or secondary glazing significantly reduces ventilation from the windows.

6. Fires are no longer in regular use or are blocked and disused. The flues may be capped at the stack, reducing ventilation.

7. The insertion of a modern concrete floor, replacing the porous floor, displaces moisture to the walls.

8. Moisture continues to enter the base of the walls from the ground.

9. The use of impervious materials, both externally and internally, entraps moisture causing salts and dampness to be displaced further up the walls.

10. The entrapment and displacement of moisture subjects the walls to prolonged dampness – increasing the risk of timbers in contact with the walls being subject to active decay.

11. Greater amounts of water vapour are produced from increased levels of cooking and bathing, particularly showers. The manner and intensity of how the building is used has dramatically changed.

12. The amount of evaporation has been significantly reduced by a decrease in the levels of ventilation. This has been brought about by the introduction of draught-excluders, secondary and double-glazing.

13. The use internally of impervious paints and finishes, provides vapour-permeable resistance, and smooth, cold, surfaces encouraging condensation from the increased levels of water vapour in the building.

14. Increased levels of condensation increase the risks of dampness, decay and mould growth. Not only is this potentially damaging for the building but is also a threat to the health of the occupants and users of the building.

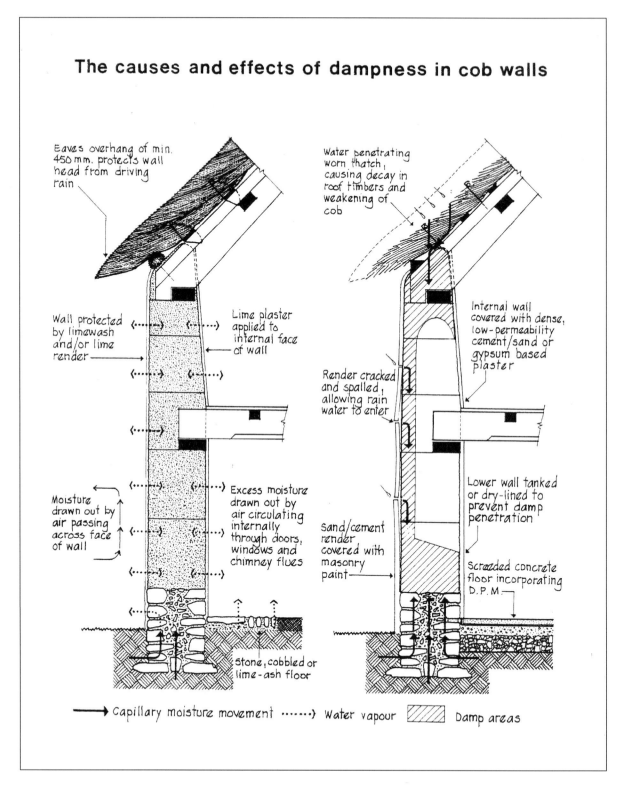

The causes and effects of dampness in cob walls

Eaves overhang of min. 450 mm. protects wall head from driving rain

Water penetrating worn thatch, causing decay in roof timbers and weakening of cob

Wall protected by limewash and/or lime render

Lime plaster applied to internal face of wall

Internal wall covered with dense, low-permeability cement/sand or gypsum based plaster

Render cracked and spalled, allowing rain water to enter

Moisture drawn out by air passing across face of wall

Excess moisture drawn out by air circulating internally through doors, windows and chimney flues

Lower wall tanked or dry-lined to prevent damp penetration

Sand/cement render covered with masonry paint

Screeded concrete floor incorporating D.P.M.

Stone, cobbled or lime-ash floor

→ Capillary moisture movement ·······› Water vapour ▨ Damp areas

Figures 5.3a and 5.3b The causes and effects of dampness in cob walls.[7] Figure 5.3a shows a wall of unaltered cob building showing how a state of moisture/air equilibrium is achieved. Figure 5.3b shows how neglect combined with inappropriate repair/maintenance can upset the balance and lead to rapid deterioration. (Kind permission of Larry Keefe)

Figure 5.4a A demonstration using a test panel of wattle and daub is a practical illustration of how traditional fabric performs in real-life conditions, and how fundamental changes to the performance influence the condition of the building.

Figure 5.4b To illustrate in a practical manner the way that traditional buildings work a panel of wattle and daub has been subjected to wetting with a garden spray. The panels represent the fabric of a building that is able to breathe.

Figure 5.4c The porous fabric absorbs the water, there is very little initial water run off. The panel is subjected to continual spraying, over and above typical conditions it would encounter in real life situations.

Figure 5.4d The water does not penetrate what are relatively thin walls, being only some four inches thick. The water continues to be absorbed until conditions allow evaporation to take place, when the panel dries out.

Figure 5.4e If the wattle and daub panel is substituted with a concrete paving slab, which represents the introduction of impervious cement rendering and/or masonry paint, a dramatic change in performance is evident.

Figure 5.4f There is immediate water run off, water exploits cracks in the panel and penetrates the fabric.

Figure 5.4g There is a build-up of water in the groove for the staves for the wattle and daub. The evaporation of the water is inhibited by the impervious finish and the timbers are subjected to prolonged dampness and eventually decay.

Figure 5.5 Such a scenario can cause serious decay to a timber-framed building, as illustrated by the condition of the horizontal rail removed from a historic timber-framed building subjected to similar conditions to those illustrated. Impervious paint had been used to repair and maintain the wall. Although the external faces of the rail are generally sound the inside of the timber is hollow, water channelled into the panel had collected in the groove for the stave and rotted the centre out.

A change in the traditional performance of a building will have a detrimental affect on its condition, as levels of damp can no longer be 'controlled'. The problems facing many other buildings are illustrated in Case Study 5.1.

Case Study 5.1 **A change in performance**

Figure 5.6a At face value the building in this case study looks like a mid-to late-twentieth-century house.

Figure 5.6b In fact this is the same building. Despite current appearances the building was originally a thatched brick and flint cottage dating from around the late eighteenth century.

The appearance and the performance of the building were dramatically changed when a comprehensive programme of modernisation was carried out in the mid 1960s. The modernisation works included re-roofing; the provision of a gable to the east elevation; raising the roofline; the removal of a chimney stack; rendering the external elevations; altering the layout of the accommodation; and the provision of modern internal finishes (plaster and floors). Replacement uPVC double glazed windows were installed in the early 1980s.

The extensive nature of the alteration work concealed the brick and flint origins of the building. The only readily available clues are the thickness of some of the walls, the exposed flintwork of the adjoining property and a photograph of the property prior to the programme of modernisation (figure 5.6b).

A survey was made of the building to assess problems of dampness. It was found that high levels of dampness were present principally for the following reasons:

- a dramatic change in the performance of the building caused by the additions of: external cement rendering, internal cement plastering, concrete floors, and double-glazed windows
- water penetration – primarily a result of failure in the external cement rendering
- lateral water penetration resulting from poor detailing, high external ground levels, the render abutting the external ground and abutting garden wall
- condensation – primarily as a result of changes in how the building is used and the lack of adequate ventilation

This building must illustrate one of the most dramatic changes in appearance and performance of a traditional building; its origins as a flint walled cottage are unrecognisable.

Figure 5.7 The levels of condensation and poor insulation detailing were causing problems of mould growth, which combined with a damp environment to have a detrimental affect on the health of the occupant.

The construction of a traditional building, therefore, should be considered as a whole and treated in a holistic way. Its structure, materials and methods of construction and patterns of air and moisture movement should be properly understood.[8]

Inappropriate repair – pointing

Even a simple recommendation can expose a building to inappropriate repair. For example, the recommendation to rake out and repoint a masonry wall can have significant impact, in both the short and long-term. Not only can serviceable fabric and evidence of previous finishes be lost but the appearance and presentation may also be changed. This will eventually affect the structural condition and the rates of decay that will be suffered.

It is important to remember that few people wittingly initiate repairs knowing that they will cause damage. The introduction of materials that are now found to be inappropriate are usually used with the intention of repairing the building.

The impact that a simple repair using inappropriate materials can have on the performance and condition of a traditional building can be illustrated where a lime-based mortar is raked out and repointed with an impervious cement mortar.

Figure 5.8 This is a graphic illustration of how the performance of a wall can be adversely affected by cement pointing. (Kind permission of the Society for the Protection of Ancient Buildings)[9]

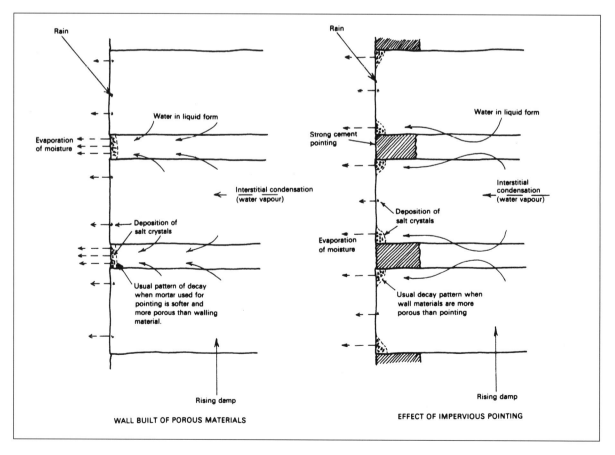

Figure 5.9 Traditionally it was common practice to ensure that the mortar was softer than the masonry. This allowed moisture to evaporate readily from the pointing rather the masonry. The pointing was looked upon as 'sacrificial' to the masonry, which is both financially and practically sensible, as the pointing is much cheaper and easier to replace than either stone or brickwork. The use of an impervious mortar that is harder than the masonry, significantly reduces the amount of moisture that can readily evaporate from the pointing, increasing the levels of moisture and salts that are attracted to the face of the masonry. This change in the nature of the material of repair has resulted in the accelerated deterioration, with the masonry becoming 'sacrificial' to the mortar.

Figure 5.10 A change in material and style of pointing can dramatically alter how a building looks.

Figure 5.11 The pointing illustrated is obviously a hard cement-based mortar, a soft lime mortar could not be picked out intact like the piece illustrated. In this case the cement pointing although well applied, with a slight recess and not buttered over the arises of the brickwork, has not been properly prepared and raked out to an adequate depth. In this instance it was possible to carefully remove the impervious cement pointing without causing excessive damage to the brickwork. Unfortunately this is not always the case.

Figure 5.12 The inherent nature of many cement mortars and renders is that they are difficult, if not impossible, to remove without causing damage to the historic fabric and, in many cases, are an irreversible intervention.

Figure 5.13 (above) Even where the correct materials have been used, in this case a lime putty based mortar, they have to be applied with a degree of skill and understanding, as the appearance of the building will only detract from the functional gains.

Figure 5.14 (right) The impervious nature of modern masonry paint is clearly reflected in the blistering of its surface where moisture and salts are trying to evaporate from the wall through the paint. Note the presence of the original limewash finish below the paint, which will assist in removing the modern masonry paint and minimise the damage to the brickwork.

Figure 5.15 (right) The impervious roofing felt has provided a barrier to the evaporation of moisture. This has resulted in condensation and mould growth and has created a damp environment conducive to wood-boring insect attack and fungal decay.

OLD BUILDINGS NEED TO BREATHE

Attempts to change the performance characteristics of a traditional 'breathing' building to those of a modern building will not be successful. The use of modern impervious materials can, at best, provide short-term solutions by cosmetically concealing the symptoms. Unless the causes are positively addressed however, the problems will eventually reappear or be displaced to another part of the building in the medium to long-term.

The use of impervious materials

As we can see, impervious materials change the performance of the building from being one that 'breathes' to one that puts a greater reliance upon preventing water/moisture from entering the fabric. Regrettably, it is exceptional to find a building that has not been subjected to some form of intervention with impervious materials. It is therefore an essential prerequisite for practitioners to be fully conversant with the problems that are likely to be encountered where there has been a detrimental change in the intended performance of a traditional building.

The well-meaning but mistaken tendency to use modern materials and methods of repair to 'protect' traditional buildings will, in most cases, lead to accelerated rates of decay. An adverse change in the performance of old buildings will create inherent problems that can, at worst, threaten the building's very existence.[10] This generation has inherited a legacy of problems that have not been faced previously, and that need to be addressed to prevent unacceptable levels of deterioration.

Case Study 5.2 Reinstating the traditional performance

Figure 5.16

A Grade II★ listed building dating from 1608 that has been in continual use as almshouses since the day it was built. Irrespective of the age and listed status of this building the construction, solid brick walls, and the problems being suffered are typical of many traditional buildings.

A condition survey identified potential problems and prioritised these for the client. One of the principal problems identified was the presence of dampness and the associated risks, of serious decay to those timbers in contact with the damp walls, and to the health of the elderly occupants. A detailed investigation into the problems of dampness enabled a repair specification to be

Figure 5.17a The impervious materials, combined with poor detailing, was allowing moisture to become entrapped in walls causing decay to window lintels, the window frames and sills.

Figure 5.17b The prolonged dampness has caused the brickwork to become very soft and spalled in areas.

produced. The introduction of impervious materials to the walls – modern masonry paints over cement slurry, cement patch repairs to spalled bricks, and cement pointing were the main causes of damp in the building.

Damp problems were evident internally and there was a long-term health risk to the elderly occupants. The threats to both the building and the occupants were reflected in the actions of the local council who provided grant aid for the works as both building conservation and environmental health projects.

The building is located in a prime location on a busy street. Not only was it required to perform well, it also had to look good when finished, to illustrate the successful use of traditional materials. The problems identified, and the demands for the building to look good once repaired, necessitated a careful assessment of the available repair options.

This was achieved by carrying out trials to find the most appropriate method of removing the paint from the walls. In this case it was found that the careful use by skilled operatives of a pressurised steam system successfully removed the plastic based paint without damaging the brickwork. The system proved to be sensitive enough to enable fragments of historic limewash finishes to be retained.

Unfortunately, the steam system did not remove the cement slurry found below the masonry paint. This could only be achieved by hand at great expense and at increased risk of damage to the brickwork. For this reason it was decided to leave the cement slurry in place on the face of the the joints of the brickwork but to carefully scrape

Figure 5.18a

Figure 5.18b

the slurry from brickwork with the intention of reinstating an area where moisture could readily evaporate from the wall. This was successfully achieved without causing any serious damage. The joints between the bricks could now to allow evaporation to take place as originally intended (see figure 5.8).

The final problem was finding a finish that would allow the evaporation of moisture from the walls, in particular the joints, and would adhere to the impervious cement slurry. In many cases traditional finishes do not adhere well to modern cement-based materials. Trials were carried out to determine what finishes would work best and also provide a satisfactory cosmetic solution.

A pure lime-putty limewash did not adhere well to the cement slurry. A casein-bound limewash – where the casein would help the limewash to adhere to the slurry – unfortunately became highly translucent when damp, and resulted in a patchwork appearance. It would not have provided a satisfactory cosmetic finish, which owing to the prominent position of the building on a busy street, was a critical consideration.

The finish that met both the performance and appearance requirements was a feebly hydraulic limewash provided with an earth pigment. This limewash adhered well to the cement slurry

providing a good cosmetic finish and still allowed the fabric to breathe.

It is always important that the client is made aware of the limitations of traditional materials, for example, that the limewashed walls darken when they get wet. Traditional materials rarely perform in a unified manner, they respond to environmental conditions particularly where there is residual damp and salts in the walls.

In this case the causes of dampness were identified and removed. The breathing performance was reinstated by using materials and methods appropriate to a traditionally constructed building. The approach was based upon an understanding of the building's performance, the detrimental changes in the traditional performance, and an understanding of the repair solutions available.

Figure 5.20 The building repaired and performing as intended.

Figure 5.19 The residual dampness in the walls can be seen to be showing through the joints of the brickwork. This reflects the success of the repair in reinstating the traditional performance and is not a problem that needs rectifying.

Essential ingredients of breathability

Three principal performance characteristics determine the breathability of a building and its fabric:

- Porosity
- Capillarity
- Hygroscopicity

Removing any one of these performance characteristics, by introducing modern materials, or even traditional materials that do not have the same performance characteristics as the original, can affect a building's ability to 'breathe'.

The importance of porosity, capillarity and hygroscopicity to the overall performance of a building has only recently been highlighted.[11,12] 'Breathability' was largely assessed upon the vapour permeability of the fabric, this perhaps has been an over simplification, because the movement of carbon dioxide through the fabric is crucial to the carbonation of lime based products.

The capillarity of building fabric dictates the ability to absorb moisture. The performance of different materials, even traditional materials, varies tremendously and can have a significant affect on the ability of the building to absorb moisture, and also its ability to dry out. Some materials, such as chalk and soft brickwork, can readily absorb moisture but cannot release it at an equivalent rate. These materials are prone to remaining damp for long periods. If evaporation has been inhibited by the introduction of modern materials, this can further delay the drying out of the fabric. The longer that these materials are subjected to dampness the greater the risks of decay. Many traditional building materials are also hygroscopic; they can absorb moisture from the atmosphere. The rate that moisture is absorbed and subsequently released is crucial in the performance of a traditional building.

It is imperative that the three principal performance characteristics (porosity, capillarity and hygroscopicity) are understood and taken into account when assessing a building's condition, and before recommending changes; to avoid disturbing what can be a complex relationship between many materials and their performance characteristics. This also illustrates the reason why replacing on a 'like for like' basis is important, as it is most likely to maintain an equilibrium in performance.

FLEXIBILITY OF OLD BUILDINGS

Shallow footings and foundations

In addition to the differences in the way modern and traditional structures deal with the movement of moisture there are also significant differences in the structural performance between traditional and modern conventional buildings.

Modern buildings are mainly rigid structures constructed on relatively deep foundations, whereas many older buildings are 'flexible' in comparison, as they do not have footings or foundations that would meet modern day standards or expectations. Older buildings are often built on very shallow footings or even directly on the soil.

> Even now there are still many symptoms of foundation failure in relatively new buildings and a vast body of older buildings showing little or no sign of trouble from this source … There is little point therefore in making comparison between new and old types of foundations as the crucial point is only whether they succeed in their purpose. Even when they fail to do so it is probably not the fault of the original foundation itself.[13]

Figure 5.21 There is obviously a problem of structural movement at this building.

Plasticity of traditional mortars

The use of lime and earth based mortars in the construction and repair of older buildings allows for some movement in the structure and seasonal variations that occur in many instances without causing structural damage. An appreciation that this 'flexibility' is an essential part of the traditional performance of many older buildings is integral to a successful inspection and survey of an historic building.

The use of soft porous lime or earth based mortars to bed the bricks or stones of a wall, not only allows moisture to evaporate from the joints, it also allows movement and initial settlement to take place in many cases without causing significant problems with cracking.

> One of the main beneficial features of lime mortars is that, being plastic rather than brittle, they are able to accept quite large deformations and distortions without the opening of bed joints or the splitting of bricks.[14]

This plasticity, the ability to allow for movement, is one of the main reasons why many old buildings survive today with all the distortions and unevenness that add considerably to their charm and character.

> Autogenous healing: When buildings made with lime are subjected to small movements they are more likely to develop many fine cracks than the individual large cracks which occur in stiffer cement-bound buildings. Water penetration into these fine cracks can dissolve 'free' lime and bring it to the surface. As the water evaporates, this lime is deposited and begins to heal the cracks. That is how some old buildings on poor foundations distort rather than fail.[15]

The skill of the person surveying older buildings lies in determining whether or not the distortion and movement suffered is a problem that warrants structural repair.

> No matter how distorted a building may be, if it is currently stable, it is in equilibrium. But equilibrium can be disturbed by unwise alteration, by serious accident, or by the introduction of heavy loading that creates, at least locally, forces beyond the building's capacity to distribute.[16]

Structural movement and underpinning

Diagnosing the actual causes of movement, reflected in distortion and cracks, can be highly complicated, and it requires great skill to strike the balance between over-reaction and complacency. Great care needs to be taken when assessing complex movement that cannot be easily diagnosed in a single inspection.

Leaning walls, cracks in masonry, etc may be symptoms of foundation settlement or other structural movement of long standing which may now have stabilised. Before any action is taken, therefore, it is necessary to understand the building structure and monitor the situation over a period of time in order to determine whether or not movement is continuing and, if it is, whether or not it is of sufficient seriousness to warrant action being taken. Monitoring should, wherever possible, be in excess of one year in order to take account of ordinary seasonal variations in movement.[17]

The standard solution often prescribed for movement to old buildings is underpinning. The application of retrospective foundations to make the building conform to the concept of a rigid structure can be an ill-advised and dangerous route to follow.

Case Study 5.3 The danger of structural works

Figure 5.22a A wychert building before structural works.

Figure 5.22b The same building after structural works.

This building collapsed during underpinning works. The building had suffered from large cracks, which may or may not have been the result of structural settlement. The repair of the building using cement renders and by building up external ground levels contributed to the base of the walls being subjected to prolonged dampness (see also Case Study 1.2). This will have resulted in the weakening of the earth in the walls, increasing the risk of slumping and failure (see figure 5.3).

The extent and nature of underpinning, even if fully justified, needs to be carefully considered, as it can be potentially dangerous. In this case, the building was in a highly sensitive state of equilibrium before the underpinning began. The principal causes of the collapse were due to a lack of appreciation of the characteristics of the building type in question (earth), or the likely consequences of proceeding with underpinning what was in effect a mud slurry wall.

Figure 5.23b (above) Underpinning is highly disruptive and irreversible. In many cases it is carried out without an understanding or appreciation of the traditional performance of older buildings and the implications of changing this performance. This wall suffered cracking that was not evident prior to the building being underpinned. The remedy can therefore cause more damage then was previously apparent.

Figure 5.23a (above) Underpinning in progress.

Figures 5.24a (left) ***and 5.24b*** (above) Excavation work to provide a new extension reveals the lack of any footings to a vernacular cottage. Alterations provide a new threat to the structural stability of a building that has stood for many centuries.

The dangers of partial underpinning need to be understood, particularly in buildings with no foundations or only shallow footings. Where underpinning provides some localised rigidity to part of a building, this can result in differential movement between those parts of the building that have now become rigid and those that remain flexible.

Timber-framed buildings are renowned for being distorted, as the jointed nature of their construction allows a greater degree of flexibility and tolerance of movement than is found in most masonry buildings. It is critical however, that great care is taken to understand the causes of the movement reflected in the distorted appearance, as alterations, such as the removal of timbers, may have allowed the building to move, while also reducing the building's structural integrity.

> ...common assaults on timber-framed buildings include removal of cross ties and piercing of infills, in both cases usually to provide opening. More often than not, the structure accommodates these alterations at the cost of some distortion and a loss of robustness, which may cause additional problems some years later.[18]

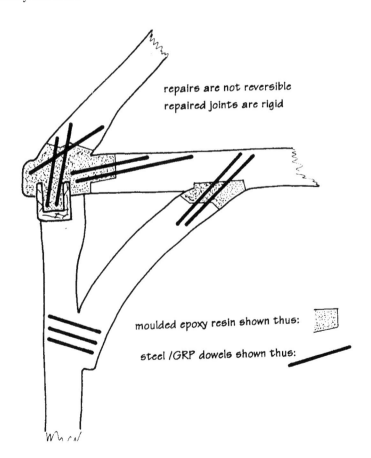

Figure 5.25 Hindering the ability of a building to move can cause problems. The once flexile joints to the timber frame are now rigid. (*Structural Repair of Traditional Buildings*[19])

In many older buildings the cracking and distortion of the walls can be complex and easily misinterpreted, and previous attempts to address the movement may be causing more problems than it solves. This is the reason that a true understanding of movement in a complex building requires a thorough knowledge of its history, and probably detailed monitoring over a lengthy period.

Case Study 5.4 Understanding the causes of movement

A Grade II★ listed building with a long and complex history had been subject to many alterations, including a significant programme of structural work in the 1960s.

A combination of documentary research, physical investigation – including soil analysis – and the interpretation of the movement and cracking, enabled the building to be understood, from the time of its original design by Robert Adam in 1778, through its many changes, including structural remedial work carried out in the 1960s.

The conclusion drawn from the extensive investigations was that the problems of movement were primarily a result of differing soil conditions.

Extensive structural works carried out in the 1960s probably exacerbated the movement, by disturbing the equilibrium of the building and subjecting it to massive disturbance.

In this case the investigations enabled an understanding of the immediate environment which allowed the formulation of a holistic approach to the repair of the building. This was achieved by using the input of a multi-disciplinary team: a structural engineer, a building historian, a surveyor acting as a historic buildings consultant, and a surveyor who undertook a detailed measured survey of the site and the building, enabling the mistakes made previously to be avoided.

Figure 5.26 Evidence of movement is readily identifiable, the distortion of the arch and masonry. But what has caused the building to move and is it still a problem?

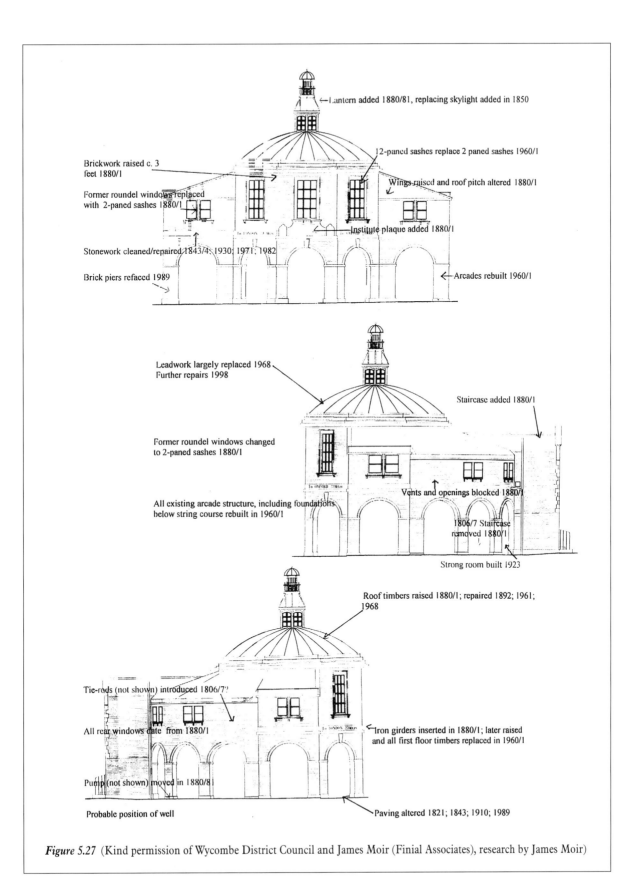

Figure 5.27 (Kind permission of Wycombe District Council and James Moir (Finial Associates), research by James Moir)

THE FLEXIBLE BREATHING BUILDING

Those inspecting and surveying traditional buildings should understand how these buildings performed as well as the potential consequences of any changes in that performance on the condition of the building. They need to know whether the materials and methods used in past programmes of repair and maintenance are compatible and consistent with the 'breathing' and 'flexible' performance of the building being inspected.

It is a relatively straightforward and simple exercise to assess the general performance of a traditional building; anyone carrying out a survey can easily recognise the warnings signs and be made aware of the likely consequences of any detrimental changes in the performance, as well as the likely overall condition of the building.

The differences between modern and traditional buildings, and the large variations within the categorisation of traditional buildings, makes it essential that the condition of any traditional building needs to be compared with buildings of a similar type. Comparison with modern equivalents that have different performance characteristics cannot be a sound basis upon which to judge the condition or specify repairs to a traditional building.

REINSTATING THE TRADITIONAL PERFORMANCE

Where the introduction of incompatible impervious materials is causing problems they should, wherever possible, be removed, but only where this will not cause more damage to the building than leaving the materials *in situ*. The appropriate removal methods should always be assessed by carrying out small trial tests. If it is found that the materials can be removed successfully and easily, without causing significant damage, this should be done with great care and usually under strict supervision. Inevitably the exposed building fabric will then require further repair, as a result of trapped moisture or the physical removal of what are usually hard materials. Once at this stage, however, it is essential that the mistakes of the past are not repeated and that only materials appropriate and consistent with the traditional construction and performance are used in the repair and future maintenance of the building.

In some cases, such as when a building has been underpinned, it will not be possible, either practically or financially, to reinstate the intended traditional performance. All advice and recommendations for repair will then need to take into account the fundamental change in the traditional performance, and warn of the threat of future problems, such as the likelihood of differential movement in the case of partial underpinning.

Predicted increases in rainfall combined with the extensive use of inappropriate impervious materials will significantly increase and accelerate future problems, caused by the entrapment of damp in the building fabric of many traditional buildings. Where the breathing capability of these buildings is not reinstated they will suffer increasingly from dampness and decay, with any deterioration of the internal environment eventually affecting the health of occupants. The problems relating to adverse changes in the intended performance of older buildings will become more relevant, with greater demands being made for repair. It is critical, however, that past mistakes are not repeated and that only compatible solutions consistent with the breathing performance of these buildings are implemented, in order to achieve the effective management of the building stock.

References

1   Hughes, P., *The Need for Old Buildings to 'Breathe'*, Information Sheet 4, The Society for the Protection of Ancient Buildings (SPAB), Spring 1986.

2   Ibid, p. 3.

3   Holmes, S. and Wingate, M., *Building with Lime*, Intermediate Technology Publications, London, 1997, p. 2.

4   Ibid, p 3.

5   Thomas, A., Williams, G. and Ashurst, N., *The Control of Damp in Old Buildings*, Technical pamphlet 8, The Society for the Protection of Ancient Buildings (SPAB), Revised and rewritten 1992.

6   Oxley, R., 'The Need For Roofs to Breathe', *The Building Conservation Directory*, Cathedral Communications, Tisbury, 2001, p. 79.

7   Bedford, P., Induni, B., Induni, E and Keefe, L., 'Appropriate Plasters, Renders and Finishes for Cob and Random Stone Walls in Devon', Devon Earth Building Association, July 1993.

8   *British Standard BS 7913: Guide to the Principles of the Conservation of Historic Buildings*, BSI, 1998, p. 8.

9   Hughes, P., *The Need for Old Buildings to 'Breathe'*, Information Sheet 4, The Society for the Protection of Ancient Buildings (SPAB), Spring 1986.

10 Oxley, R., 'Mistaken protection', *SPAB News*, Vol. 20, No. 2, 1999.

11 Minke, G., *Earth Construction Handbook: The building material earth in modern architecture*, WIT Press, Southampton, 2000.

12 May, N., Paper submitted at the Building Limes Forum, Edinburgh, 2001.

13 Melville, I.A. and Gordon, I.A., *The Repair and Maintenance of Houses*, The Estates Gazette, London, 1997, p. 116.

14 *Structural Renovation of Traditional Buildings*, CIRIA Report 111, London, 1986.

15 Holmes, S. and Wingate, M., *Building with Lime*, Intermediate Technology Publications, London, 1997, p. 3.

16 Robson, P., *Structural Repair of Traditional Buildings*, Donhead, Shaftesbury, 1999, p. 108.

17 Brereton, C., *The Repair of Historic Buildings: Advice on principles and methods*, English Heritage, London, 1991, p. 18.

18 Robson, P., *Structural Repair of Traditional Buildings*, Donhead, Shaftesbury, 1999, p. 108.

19 Ibid, p. 196.

6 | LEGISLATION

PROTECTION OF HISTORIC BUILDINGS

The practitioner needs to be aware that many older buildings may be statutorily protected and controlled, because they are:

- listed, and/or
- situated in a conservation area, or
- scheduled as ancient monuments

It would not be professional, or wise, for a practitioner to make recommendations without identifying whether a building is protected, or to provide advice or recommendations without understanding the practical implications of that protection.

The highly complex and specialised area of statutory protection means that this chapter can act only as an introductory guide. For this reason certain key issues have been selected that are thought to be particularly relevant to the inspection of traditional buildings.

Controlling legislation will differ from country to country and any assessment of a protected building, or any advice given, will need to reflect the controls relevant to each individual country. It is also important to remember that each building needs to be assessed on its individual merits.

This chapter is based upon current legislation relevant to buildings in England and Wales, primarily the Planning (Listed Buildings and Conservation Areas) Act 1990, but the legislation in Scotland – the Planning (Listed Buildings and Conservation Areas) (Scotland) Act 1997 – is very similar in its intent and application. More detailed sources of information, such as PPG 15 in England and Wales; and books and journals can offer supplementary guidance in this area.[1,2,3]

Before looking at the detail it is important to appreciate why special protection is given to many historic buildings:

It is fundamental to the Government's policies for environmental stewardship that there should be effective protection for all aspects of the historic environment. The physical survivals of our past are to be valued and protected for their own sake, as a central part of our cultural heritage and our sense of national identity. They are an irreplaceable record which contributes, through formal education and in many other ways, to our understanding of both the present and the past. Their presence adds to the quality of our lives by enhancing the familiar and cherished local scene and sustaining the sense of local distinctiveness which is so important an aspect of the character and appearance of our towns, villages and countryside. The historic environment is also of immense importance for leisure and recreation.[4]

The rationale behind the protection is that, once lost, historic buildings cannot be replaced. They represent a finite resource and an irreplaceable asset and for this reason there should be a general presumption in favour of their preservation.

SCHEDULED ANCIENT MONUMENTS

There are a relatively limited number of scheduled ancient monuments, many being in the care and ownership of organisations such as English Heritage or Historic Scotland. It is unlikely that the average practitioner will encounter these buildings and structures on a regular basis. It is usually structures such as ruins, and ancient sites – many subterranean – rather than buildings, that are statutorily protected as scheduled ancient monuments.

Under the Ancient Monuments and Archaeological Areas Act 1979, scheduled monument consent is required for almost any works, including repair, affecting a scheduled monument. In particular consent is required for:

Any works resulting in:
- the demolition or destruction of a scheduled monument
- any damage to it

Any works for the purpose of:
- removing or repairing a scheduled monument or any part of it
- making any alterations or additions to it; and

Any flooding or tipping operations on land in, or under which there is a scheduled monument

The responsibility for control of scheduled ancient monuments lies with the Secretaries of State and their expert advisers, rather than with local planning authorities.

Figures 6.1a and 6.1b
Notification and
approval was required
for the urgent propping
works provided to this
scheduled ancient
monument. A full
application for consent
was required for the
structural repair work as
illustrated in figure
6.1b.

Carrying out unauthorised work to a scheduled ancient monument, or the land upon which it stands, is a criminal offence, so consent needs to be obtained before recommending or implementing any work to a scheduled ancient monument. This includes minor repairs work such as repointing.

The implications of a building or structure being scheduled are restrictive, consequently a practitioner has a professional responsibility to advise the existing owner or anyone intending to purchase a scheduled monument (or a building with a scheduled monument on its grounds) of the limitations in force. Failure to do so has the potential to expose the monument to irreparable damage and the client, and/or the practitioner, to criminal prosecution, should inappropriate and unauthorised works be carried out.

LISTED BUILDINGS

A listed building is the type of individually protected building that is most likely to be encountered. There are three grades for buildings on the statutory lists, Grades I, II★ and II. Grades I and II★ comprise only a small proportion, (approximately six per cent) of all listed buildings. These grades identify those buildings of outstanding architectural or historical interest that are particularly important to the nation's built heritage; their significance will generally be beyond dispute. Ninety-four per cent of all listed buildings are Grade II and are recognised as being of special architectural or historic interest.

Figure 6.2 Some buildings can be readily identified as being listed. In this case the owner is proud to declare the listed status. Hopefully the owner is not so proud of the use of cement mortar to repoint the building.

It can sometimes be difficult to recognise whether a building is listed or not, and the inspecting practitioner needs to be aware of the potential influence of statutory protection. There can, for example, be instances where it is a surprise to find that a building is listed, as it is relatively modern, conversely some very old buildings are not listed.

The list of buildings that are protected is constantly amended, with buildings being added and removed from the list on a daily basis. The only definitive way of determining whether a building is listed, is a scheduled ancient monument, or is situated in a conservation area, is to make enquiries of either the local authority planning department, many of which have dedicated conservation officers, or the Historic Buildings Inspectorate (English Heritage, Historic Scotland, Cadw, or the Department of Environment in Northern Ireland).

In light of the statutory protection afforded listed buildings, and the implications this can have for the survey and subsequent alterations or 'repairs' it is common sense to find out whether or not a building is protected before making an inspection. It is equally important to ensure that the inspecting practitioner has the appropriate skills and knowledge to assess and report on that particular building, rather than risk having to readjust the approach, advice and recommendations retrospectively.

Criteria for listing

In certain situations there will be a need to determine on site the likelihood of a building being protected. In these circumstances the criteria for listing that are applied when deciding which buildings to include in the statutory lists provide a useful guide.

Architectural interest: the lists are meant to include all buildings which are of importance to the nation for the interest of their architectural design, decoration and craftsmanship; also important examples of particular building types and techniques (e.g. buildings displaying technological innovation or virtuosity) and significant plan forms;

Historic interest: this includes buildings which illustrate important aspects of the nation's social, economic or military history;
Close historical association: with nationally important people or events;
Group value: especially where buildings comprise an important architectural or historic unity or a fine example of planning (eg. squares, terraces or model villages).[5]

In addition, the age and rarity of a building are also relevant to assessing the likelihood of whether it is listed or not. PPG 15 provides specific guidance in this respect that can be helpful to the practitioner:

...all buildings built before 1700 which survive in anything like their original condition are listed; and most buildings of 1700 to 1840 are listed, though some selection is necessary. After about 1840, because of the greatly increased number of buildings erected and the much larger numbers that have survived, greater selection is necessary to identify the best examples of particular building types [and] only buildings of definite quality and character are listed. For the same reasons only selected buildings from the period after 1914 are normally listed. Buildings which are less than 30 years old are normally listed only if they are of exceptional quality and under threat. Buildings which are less than ten years old are not listed.[6]

Put simply, any building dating wholly or in part from 1840 or earlier is likely to have historic importance and therefore be listed.

List description

The list description is usually very brief, commonly a single sentence or paragraph describing the building. This assessment is usually based upon an external inspection and it is therefore wise to adopt a degree of caution when referring to it because in some cases the listing can be incorrect. The list description also provides background information that may, or may not, assist in determining the special interest of the building. It can only be used as an introduction to a building and will, in most cases, indicate why the building was listed in the first place.

Figure 6.3

In this example the listed building is described as:

> Building of circa 1700, much restored. Irregular shaped. Left hand section of 2 storeys and attic, 2 windows, has sash windows with glazing bars in near-flush, moulded frames. Taller, right hand section of 2 storeys and attic, 2 windows. The windows of similar type, except that ground and 1st floor right hand ones are of 3 lights. High pitched, tiled roof has 2 hipped gables to front, and 2 square dormers. Steps to renewed door with moulded architrave and bracketed cornice hood. 2-storey, one window extension at left.

The list description was apparently made from an external inspection, as it does not identify the exposed smoke-blackened roof timbers, including crown posts, indicative of the building having origins as a medieval open hall house and therefore being much earlier than 1700 as suggested in the list description. Dendro-chronology (tree-ring dating) of the internal timber frame of 1418–1419 and the smoke-blackened roof timbers have provided information that confirms the early fifteenth-century origins of the building.

Figure 6.4

It is not unknown for buildings that have not been listed to be found worthy of listing after an internal inspection or building works have been initiated. In this case the building was purchased as an unlisted building situated in a conservation area that was thought to be of Victorian origin. Opening up works by a builder revealed a timber-framed building behind the façade, including the remnants of a smoke-blackened crown post.

An archaeological assessment of the timbers and dendro-chronology (tree-ring dating) revealed the building to date from between 1279–1299 and likely to be the earliest known building of its type in England. As a result this building was given a Grade II★ listing to reflect its national importance.

The extent and nature of controls

It is commonly thought that there are greater powers of control over a Grade I rather than a Grade II listed building. This is not the case. The legislation does not differentiate in the implementation or its interpretation, the level of protection is the same for all listed buildings, irrespective of their grade. It is also a common misconception to believe that the listing covers only the frontage or exterior of a building, or only items mentioned in the list description. In fact, the whole of the building is protected, both externally and internally; this includes modern extensions physically attached to the building and internal features that are an essential part of the building's character.

Figure 6.5 (right) This finely embossed gilded Lincrusta wallpaper, dating from around 1880, forms part of the special interest of a listed building. Its removal would therefore require listed building consent. In this case the paper was cleaned, consolidated and missing sections recreated, so that the decorative scheme could be reinstated.

Figures 6.6a and 6.6b (below) The modern extension to the listed building is also listed; any works that affect the character of the building, such as demolition of the extension, will require listed building consent even though it can be argued that the extension itself is of no special architectural or historic interest.

Listed building controls apply to works that would affect a building's special architectural or historic interest. Consent is normally required for demolition, in whole or in part, and for any works of alteration or extension, which would affect its character. Consent is not normally required for repairs, except where repairs involve alterations that would affect the character of the building. Whether repairs actually constitute alterations that require consent must be determined in each case. Consent should be sought from the local planning authority.

One of the main reasons why practitioners must determine whether a building is protected or not is that there are strict controls in place, including enforcement and prosecution procedures. Section 7 of the 1990 Act states:

> No person shall execute or cause to be executed any works for the
> demolition of a listed building or for its alteration or extension in any
> manner which would affect its character as a building of special architectural
> or historic merit.
>
> If a person contravenes section 7 he shall be guilty of an offence.
> (Section 9 of the 1990 Act)

It is important to note the phrase *cause to be executed* as it is rarely practitioners who actually physically carry out, or execute, the work. They are, however, primarily responsible for causing works to be executed by making recommendations or specifications for repair.

As it is a criminal offence to carry out works without consent, it is essential that practitioners identify whether a building is listed, have an understanding of the implications of any protection, and also protect against potential exposure to criminal prosecution. The practitioner needs to be aware of the possibility that works may have already been carried out without consent and are therefore unauthorised, as well as the dangers of making recommendations for works that require consent. Typical examples of unauthorised work encountered, as the works would require listed building consent, include:

- the replacement of windows; timber sashes replaced by uPVC double glazed units
- the replacement of roof coverings with materials that do not match the existing, e.g. changing from handmade clay tiles to modern concrete tiles
- the removal of internal partitions and plaster finishes
- the replacement of historic floors with modern equivalents; brick pavers or stone flags replaced with a solid concrete floor
- the removal of renders and plasters to expose brick or stonework or to facilitate remedial damp-proofing work

The use of modern materials to repair or alter a listed building will not usually be acceptable. Traditional styles, materials and construction methods are strongly encouraged, such as the use of traditional lime mortars to repoint and re-render historic buildings.

Repair or alteration?

In general there is a need for consent for alteration, but not repair, to a listed building, although in some cases there is a fine distinction between the two and it is clearly important to make the distinction. Work that perhaps would normally be classified as a repair, but in the case of a listed building would be classified as an alteration includes: the removal of original materials such as lath and plaster, or wattle and daub, and their replacement with modern alternatives, such as expanded metal lath or plasterboard. The repainting of the exterior of a listed building in different colours and the cleaning of brickwork, stone and timber using abrasive methods may also require consent.

Outbuildings, structures and curtilage issues

There are many potential pitfalls for the unwary practitioner, such as dismissing as unimportant a dilapidated barn that stands in the grounds of a listed building.

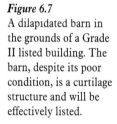

Figure 6.7
A dilapidated barn in the grounds of a Grade II listed building. The barn, despite its poor condition, is a curtilage structure and will be effectively listed.

Any freestanding building or structure within the curtilage of a listed building that was built before 1 July 1948 is also afforded protection, and is effectively listed. For this reason, even where the practitioner has identified that the barn is not listed in its own right, he needs to be aware that he cannot ignore the condition of other buildings on the land as there can be serious implications for the owner.

Curtilage structures include boundary walls, outbuildings and garden ornaments. The definition of the curtilage of a building is a complex matter that can be summarised as: land that has had a close and contiguous relationship with the listed building over many years. These unlisted structures are effectively listed by virtue of being situated within the curtilage of a listed building, all have their own potential repairing liabilities, illustrating the importance of correctly assessing the condition of all 'curtilage' buildings and structures from the outset.

Enforcement notices

Where work is carried out without consent a local planning authority can issue a listed building enforcement notice. The notice may:

- require the building to be brought back to its former state; or
- if that is not reasonably practicable or desirable, require other works specified in the notice to alleviate the effects of the unauthorised works; or
- require the building to be brought back into the state it would have been in if the terms of any listed building consent had been observed

It is not often appreciated that there are no time restrictions on when an enforcement notice can be served. Where unauthorised alterations have been made to a building the responsibility for rectifying these lies with the present owner. If the title of the building transfers to a new owner it is the new owner who becomes responsible for putting the works right. New owners technically acquire liability for past unauthorised work. Although they cannot be prosecuted, enforcement action is still possible.

The practitioner must therefore assess what alterations have been made since the building was listed, and whether the necessary consents and approvals were obtained. If the works are found to be unauthorised there is the potential for retrospective action, where the new owners are forced to remedy the situation to the satisfaction of the local planning authority. The potential financial implications of unauthorised works can be relatively substantial.

Case Study 6.1 Unauthorised works

Figure 6.8

A mortgage valuation carried out during the purchase of this building identified that the building was listed. The valuer used a standard phrase to reflect the building's listed status: 'I understand that the property is a listed building. This may affect future repairs or alterations and you may/will need specialist advice.' The valuer did not however mention that the building had been

subjected to extensive modernisation, nor did the valuer recommend that it be determined if alterations made during the modernisation works obtained and complied with the necessary consents and approvals.

The works to the building included:

- the provision of dormers
- rendering and painting the external elevations (with a dense cement render and modern masonry paint)

The calculated cost of reinstating the building back to a condition that was acceptable to the conservation officer, so that retrospective listed building consent would be granted, was approximately 50 per cent of the building's open market value on the assumption the building was in a good condition.

This case illustrates that listed status, combined with the unauthorised works carried out, affected the material value of the building and had potential financial implications for the purchaser and the practitioner.

Repairs notices

Local authorities also have the power to take action where a listed building has deteriorated to the extent that its preservation may be at risk. These powers include serving a repair notice on the owner if they consider that a listed building is not being properly preserved, here protracted failure by an owner to keep a listed building in reasonable repair places the building at risk. If the notice is not complied with, the authority may compulsorily purchase the building.

Urgent works

Local authorities, and English Heritage in Greater London, can execute any works that appear to them to be urgently necessary for the preservation of a listed building. If a building is occupied, the works may be carried out only to those parts of the building not in use. These powers can be applied to an unlisted building in a conservation area, if its preservation is important for maintaining the character or appearance of the area.[7]

Figure 6.9

A listed building that has already been subject to temporary urgent works. These have deteriorated and the building is in such a condition that additional urgent works are deemed necessary by the local planning authority to prevent further deterioration.

A schedule of urgent works is drafted and served upon the owner. The owner has to comply with these or the local planning authority has the power to carry out the work and recoup the costs from the owner.

The cost implications, and the fact that a legal charge will be registered on the land, illustrate the importance of correctly evaluating the condition of a building and understanding the implication of the controlling legislation and the responsibilities and potential liabilities of owners.

CONSERVATION AREAS

Practitioners will most commonly encounter buildings that are protected because they are situated in a conservation area. The power to designate conservation areas was introduced in 1967, in order to control the appearance and character of those areas, and there are now almost 10,000 in total in the United Kingdom. Within a conservation area a local authority has extra controls over demolition, minor development and the protection of trees. Designation introduces a general control over the demolition of unlisted buildings and provides the basis for policies designed to preserve or enhance all aspects of character or appearance that define an area's special interest.

Applications are required for consent to demolish any building within a conservation area. There is generally a presumption in favour of retaining buildings that make a positive contribution to the character or appearance of the area. Minor developments are controlled to ensure that any alterations do not detract from the conservation area's appearance. These changes may include certain types of cladding, inserting dormer windows and even putting up satellite dishes visible from the street.

Article 4 directives

A local planning authority may wish to protect certain characteristics of a conservation area that could be eroded by works carried out as permitted development. The local authority would have no control, as planning permission is not required over works carried out as permitted development. The method of control available to the local authority in these circumstances is an Article 4 directive, as conservation area status alone does not provide the scope for stringent control, particularly in comparison with the controls in place for scheduled monuments and listed buildings. It is only where there is an Article 4 directive in force that the controls can start to take more effect.

An Article 4 directive can remove certain permitted development rights in respect of minor works for which a planning application is not normally required but that affect certain aspects of the external appearance. These typically include matters such as the construction of small extensions to dwelling houses, the painting of external elevations, doors, windows, roofs and frontages. Not all conservation areas have these, but where they are in force they do influence the extent and nature of alteration that can take place to an unlisted building within a conservation area.

Permitted development rights are mainly relevant to dwelling houses. Some types of building, such as blocks of flats and commercial premises do not have permitted development rights and Article 4 directions do not therefore apply.

Figure 6.10

A typical late Victorian mid-terrace house. Anyone inspecting this building would need to be aware that although it is an unlisted building it is located in a conservation area with an Article 4 directive in force.

Although a relatively common type of building it is protected, and certain permitted development rights have been removed; in this case alterations to: front roof slopes; rainwater goods and gutters; windows and doors; brickwork (the painting of brickwork is prohibited) and front boundaries.

A lack of awareness of the controls could have serious implications for the special qualities and characteristics of the building, the designated conservation area, and the owner, potential purchaser or the practitioner.

A recent decision in the House of Lords (Shimizu UK Ltd v. Westminster City Council) defined the difference between demolition and alteration of unlisted buildings in conservation areas and where there was no Article 4 direction in force.[8]

Prior to the decision in the House of Lords it was thought that partial demolition required conservation area consent. As a result of the decision in the Shimizu case conservation area consent is only required for work that involves the total or substantial destruction of an unlisted building in a conservation area and not for alteration or extension. For example, the removal of an entire building leaving only the façade, or the removal of an entire front garden wall may require conservation area consent. This means that many works which involve the destruction of only a part of the fabric of a building will not be considered to be works of demolition, and as such will not require conservation area consent.[9]

Examples of where conservation area consent would not be required for an unlisted building in a conservation area include the removal of:

- a single window
- a whole shop front
- one wall of a building
- a porch
- the knocking of hole in wall prior to extension
- or the removal of architectural details such as finials, gate-piers etc

These alterations may however require planning permission. The principal controls in a conservation area relate to development, for example, the erection of outbuildings greater than 10m³ needs planning permission.

Trees

In the case of trees, there are controls over cutting down or carrying out works in conservation areas, whether or not a Tree Preservation Order protects the tree. Notice has to be given to the local authority so that due consideration can be given to the contribution the tree makes to the character of the area and if necessary, whether a Tree Preservation Order is required.

This means that trees, subject to certain exceptions (trees with a trunk diameter less than 75 mm at a height of 1.5 metres above ground level, ones that are dead, dying or dangerous) in conservation areas are given some protection, and anyone proposing to fell, top or lop a tree in a conservation area must give six weeks' notice to the local planning authority.

THE IMPLICATIONS OF LEGISLATION

There is a fundamental requirement for those surveying older buildings to have an appreciation of the potential for a building to be protected, and to understand the practical, legal and financial implications of any protection.

There is a need to establish what work, if any, has occurred between the time when a structure received protected status and the present. If the survey reveals indications that a protected building has been worked upon relatively recently it is clearly desirable to establish that consent (if needed) was given and that the execution of the works was as approved.

The practitioner has a duty to advise a client (the owner, purchaser, lender, solicitors) that there is a planning constraint, with potentially serious legal implications, that can materially affect the value of a building and influence its future repair and alteration. Simply having its address should be sufficient information to determine its status – is it scheduled, listed or in a conservation area.

References

1 Department of the Environment/Department of National Heritage, *Planning Policy Guidance Note 15, Planning and the Historic Environment*, HMSO, London, 1994 (at the time of writing PPG15 is under review).

2 Mynors, C., *Listed Buildings. Conservation Areas and Monuments*, Sweet & Maxwell, London, 1999.

3 *Context*, the publication of the Institute of Historic Building Conservation.

4 Department of the Environment/Department of National Heritage, *Planning Policy Guidance Note 15, Planning and the Historic Environment*, HMSO, London, 1994, section 1.1.

5 Ibid, Principles of selection, 6.10, pp. 26–7.

6 Ibid, Principles of selection, 6.11, p. 27.

7 *Stopping the Rot*, English Heritage, London. May 1998.

8 Shimizu (UK) Ltd v. Westminster City Council (1997) 1 W.L.R. 168; [197] 1 All E.R. 481.

9 Office of the Deputy Prime Minister, Department for Culture, Media and Sport. DETR Circular 01/2001. Culture, Media and Sport. Circular 01/2001. Arrangements for handling heritage applications – Notifications and Directions by the Secretary of State. Appendix D Implications of the House of Lords Judgment in the case of Shimizu (UK) Ltd v Westminster City Council.

ASSESSMENT OF THE BUILDING

7

Any responsible assessment will have to take account of not only what is seen to survive, but what might actually survive beneath the present surface, or what one might expect to find, given the age of the particular building and the conventions of that day.[1]

The following concentrates on what needs to be included in any assessment for survey and repair of a traditional building over and above what would be expected for a modern building. It is not a definitive list, as some buildings will require in depth research and analysis whilst others may need only a brief overview.

Not every historic building or landscape subject to a proposal for repair, development or alteration requires fully detailed analysis before a decision can be made. The skill of the conservation adviser lies in knowing when further information is required, and being able to match the type of information and also the amount of information to the particular case.[2]

Perhaps the biggest difference between the survey and repair of traditional and modern buildings is the amount of time required. In the case of traditional structures, more time is needed to get a feel for the building, its character, and its many changes, to reflect on the complex and sometimes contradictory findings, and to evaluate and follow the thread of reasoning in order to arrive at rational conclusions.

Each building should be evaluated on its individual merits; there can be no standard or prescriptive approach. A full assessment may be too detailed or sophisticated for some buildings, while for others a full in-depth assessment is justified because of its importance or the complexity encountered. It will take less time to gain a thorough understanding of a typical Victorian mid-terrace building than a medieval building that has been subject to alteration and adaptation throughout its long history.

Every building should be approached with an open and analytical mind. It is important to not only assess the building in the three-dimensional world within which it currently stands, but also to consider the impact of the past whilst anticipating the sustainable approach needed in the future.

> He must work in four dimensions; length, breadth, height and time, i.e. the history of the site, of any previous buildings and of how the present building came into being and has and will react to the forces of decay.[3]

If a survey is rushed and based on an approach that does not reflect the individual character of the building, it is very unlikely that the condition, the decay mechanisms, and the need for repair will be understood. The survey will fail in its purpose, as it will have assessed the building out of context of its surroundings, its history, its special interest, its development, the changes that have been made, and how it was and is being used. Any recommendations or repair solutions devised in these circumstances will be made in isolation from the very qualities that make that building unique. Standard methods of inspection, surveying or reporting will be found wanting.

Each building is unique. A comparison of several terraced Victorian buildings in the same street will reveal that each has been subjected to a different degree of alteration, extension and repair. They will each have their own particular problems, possibly related to microclimates, exposure to prevailing winds, varying degrees of inappropriate repair and maintenance, and different usage. Any building that has stood for a period of time will have developed characteristics of an individual nature.

The inter-relationship between a building and its immediate surroundings is fundamental to understanding the building's original purpose, and its function. The problems of how it stands in the landscape, for example as a result of being built into sloping ground, situated next to a river or on an exposed site are also important.

Figure 7.1 A water mill taking advantage of a site that provides a plentiful supply of water, a sloping site for gravity, and a mill pond. But this site, by its very nature, is prone to flooding and high levels of dampness. The site presented opportunities that the intended use exploited, but also provided problems for the building and the occupants.

MICROCLIMATES

Each individual building may have a number of microclimates. Most churches have an east–west orientation that exposes the north and south elevations to very different climates. The north receives little or no sunlight but escapes the extremes of weather from prevailing south-westerly winds. North walls can be subjected to prolonged dampness, as they do not receive the benefit of a drying sun and are usually sheltered. South-facing walls are usually exposed to prevailing winds and extremes in temperature. Consequently, timbers in contact with north-facing walls, particularly thick masonry walls, are vulnerable to decay.

A south-facing wall can suffer from accelerated rates of decay caused by fluctuations in temperature and regular wetting and drying cycles. Whereas a north-facing wall is subjected to fewer fluctuations as the environmental conditions are more stable, this is usually reflected in its condition. The detailing of a building can itself create microclimates that may cause problems and exacerbate local conditions.

Figures 7.2a and 7.2b The north elevation of the church can be seen to be in shade. There is an area to the north wall between the west of the porch and a buttress that is very sheltered and receives no direct sunlight and very little air movement. The dripping eaves are providing a regular and significant source of dampness. The microclimate created between the porch and buttress, together with significant amounts of water, is preventing the wall from drying out. This is causing excessive algal and lichen growth and a problem of dampness internally.

Figures 7.3a and 7.3b The inspection of this building revealed that moisture retention by the tile creasing and weathering detail above the first floor window was contributing to the accelerated deterioration of the earth blocks immediately above it. The area in question is in the south-east corner of the building. The east wing of the adjoining building overshadows and cuts out sunlight, particularly in the winter months and the corner is sheltered from south-westerly winds. The resulting microclimate is preventing the tiles from drying out, and causing dampness and deterioration to the building fabric.

THE PLAN OF THE BUILDING

The plan, the footprint and floorplan, of a building are an integral part of its special interest. Understanding the plan and how a building has developed will inform the practitioner of alterations that have been made to accommodate physical changes to the building.[4]

The most effective way of gaining an understanding of the plan and form of a building is to have floor plans drawn up (preferably from a measured survey). Sketching floor plans is often seen as a time-consuming exercise, but is one that reaps dividends for the practitioner as it significantly improves the understanding of a building and assists in following the trail of potential defects. Concealed voids and potential problems, such as the lack of adequate support where walls or chimney breasts have been removed, can be more readily identified. A complex jigsaw, often with many pieces missing, can be put together when plans are available.

The drawing of plans can also assist in enabling the relatively complex information collated on site to be recorded easily and interpreted for future use. Simple block plans or sketch elevations made on site using a limited number of measurements, to provide a degree of scale, can be incorporated into a report. This not only enhances the practitioner's understanding of the building but also that of the client and where necessary, the building contractor.

Figure 7.4a (left) Gable to a timber-framed building.

Figure 7.4b (below) A simple sketch of the timber-frame assists in identifying and understanding the problems.

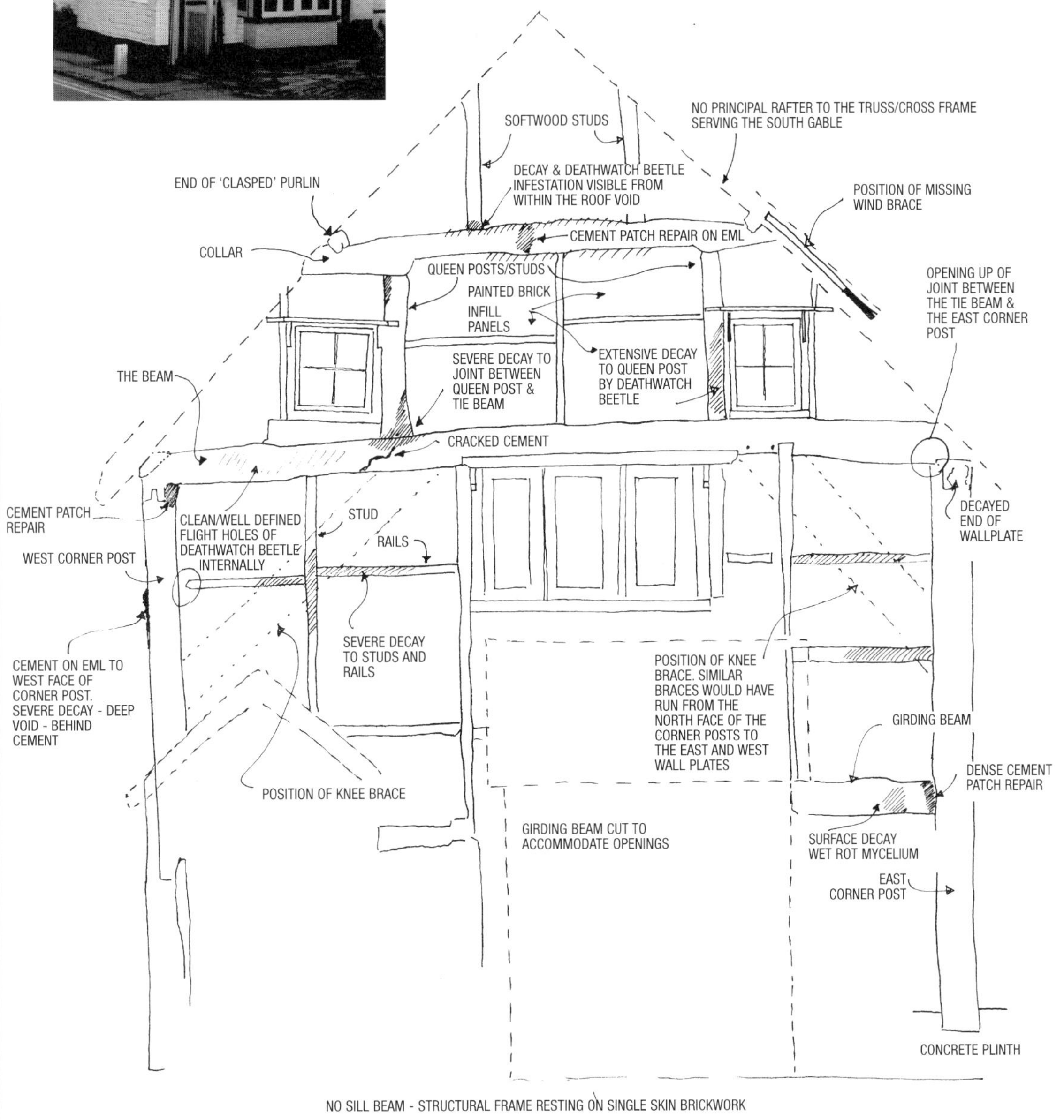
SOFTWOOD STUDS
NO PRINCIPAL RAFTER TO THE TRUSS/CROSS FRAME SERVING THE SOUTH GABLE
DECAY & DEATHWATCH BEETLE INFESTATION VISIBLE FROM WITHIN THE ROOF VOID
END OF 'CLASPED' PURLIN
POSITION OF MISSING WIND BRACE
CEMENT PATCH REPAIR ON EML
COLLAR
QUEEN POSTS/STUDS
OPENING UP OF JOINT BETWEEN THE TIE BEAM & THE EAST CORNER POST
PAINTED BRICK
INFILL PANELS
SEVERE DECAY TO JOINT BETWEEN QUEEN POST & TIE BEAM
EXTENSIVE DECAY TO QUEEN POST BY DEATHWATCH BEETLE
THE BEAM
CRACKED CEMENT
CEMENT PATCH REPAIR
DECAYED END OF WALLPLATE
CLEAN/WELL DEFINED FLIGHT HOLES OF DEATHWATCH BEETLE INTERNALLY
STUD
RAILS
WEST CORNER POST
SEVERE DECAY TO STUDS AND RAILS
CEMENT ON EML TO WEST FACE OF CORNER POST. SEVERE DECAY - DEEP VOID - BEHIND CEMENT
POSITION OF KNEE BRACE. SIMILAR BRACES WOULD HAVE RUN FROM THE NORTH FACE OF THE CORNER POSTS TO THE EAST AND WEST WALL PLATES
GIRDING BEAM
DENSE CEMENT PATCH REPAIR
POSITION OF KNEE BRACE
GIRDING BEAM CUT TO ACCOMMODATE OPENINGS
SURFACE DECAY WET ROT MYCELIUM
EAST CORNER POST
CONCRETE PLINTH
NO SILL BEAM - STRUCTURAL FRAME RESTING ON SINGLE SKIN BRICKWORK

THE DEVELOPMENT OF THE BUILDING

A thorough understanding of the historic development of a building or monument is a necessary preliminary to its repair.[5]

Figure 7.5
Cross-section of timber frame showing development of building from 13th century. (Kind permission of Barrie Norman & Steve Hext, drawing by Mike Dunn/BEAMS)

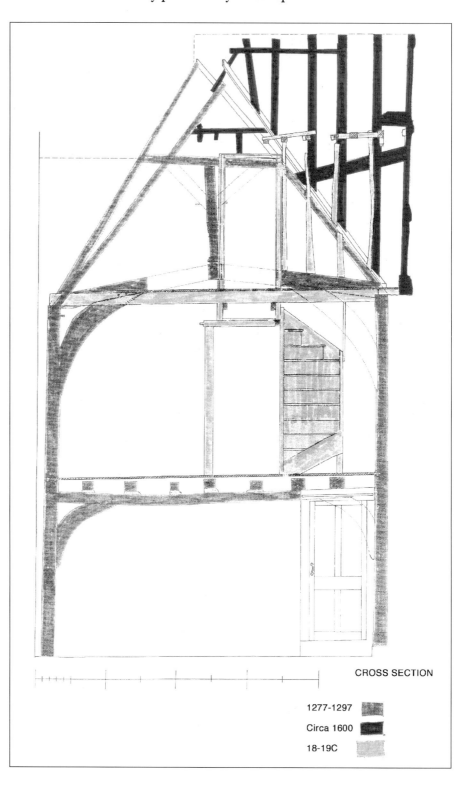

CROSS SECTION

1277-1297
Circa 1600
18-19C

Many traditional buildings have been subject to so many alterations and changes over the centuries, that, in some cases, the original core of a building is lost.

A straightforward addition onto the rear or flank of a building is readily recognisable. Untangling a history of development in an older building is rarely this straightforward, and it can be difficult and onerous, but is a task that is essential to achieving an understanding of a building.

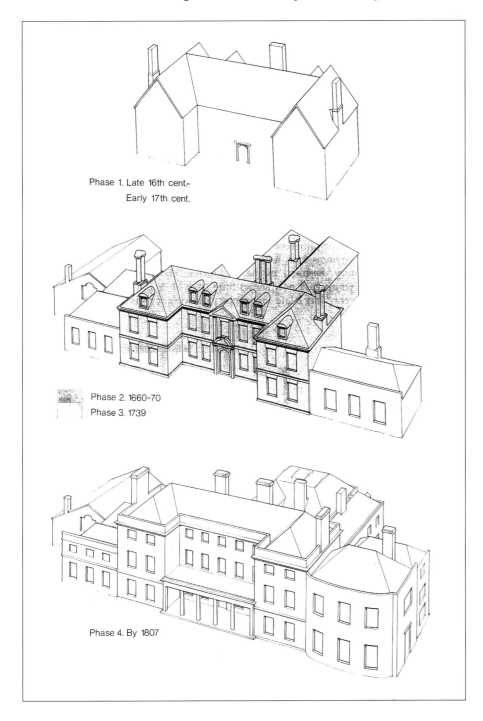

Phase 1. Late 16th cent.- Early 17th cent.

Phase 2. 1660-70
Phase 3. 1739

Phase 4. By 1807

Figure 7.6
Newsells Park, Barkway: development perspectives.
(*English Houses – The Hertfordshire Evidence* Crown copyright NMR)

Case Study 7.1 Historical development

Understanding the historical development of a building can assist in identifying the cause of a problem and the repair solutions available. In historic buildings it is important that the significance of the building fabric is also understood so that informed decisions can be made that minimise its loss.

In this case severe roof spread had occurred and was ongoing. Some of the roof timbers in this building are smoke blackened; probably reflecting the building had origins as a medieval open-hall. The roof had been subject to various programmes of repair and alteration. The front and rear wallplates had been altered and cut to accommodate the first floor windows. Established alterations had been made to the original roof using elm, and more 'recent' repairs, probably Victorian in origin, had been carried out using pine.

The history of repair and alteration together with a past failure – the front elm purlin had dropped by some 26 inches (650 mm) and had cracked at mid-point – had contributed to the problem of roof spread. Extensive firring, (the fixing of timber to the upper surfaces of the rafters to provide a uniform level to overcome sagging) of the roof had been provided to try and provide even slopes.

Understanding the development of the roof frame enabled the problems associated with each period to be determined and appropriate repair solutions to be successfully devised.

The repairs had to reinstate the structural performance of the roof whilst minimising the loss of historic fabric. This was achieved by removing the later Victorian softwood repairs, as they were not performing a structural function. Their removal made room for a new structural frame to be installed. The decision to remove the Victorian softwood timbers was not taken lightly, but in this case it was essential to facilitate the repair of the roof. The historic smoke-blackened and elm timbers were retained, and a new softwood frame was built over and through the retained timbers. Lateral restraint was provided by timber collars and metal bars.

Figure 7.7b Structural joints had failed.

Figure 7.7a (above left) The severity of the roof spread is visible to the eaves reflected in the bulging in the wall.

Figure 7.7d (above right) The roof in the process of repair – the Victorian softwood timbers have been removed to make room for the new structural frame, which includes collars and metal straps to improve the lateral restraint.

Figure 7.7c The slope of the roof had been all but lost at the eaves, allowing water penetration and resultant decay of the elm wallplate.

Documentary and physical investigation can assist in understanding the development of a building. In this case the building is the amalgamation of two separate buildings.

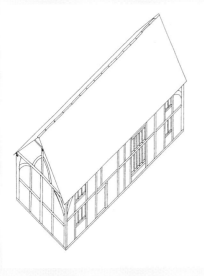
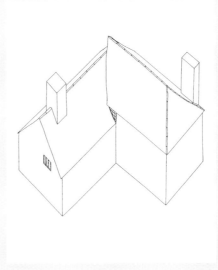

Figure 7.8a (left) Interpretation of the medieval hall denro-dated to 1418–19.

Figure 7.8b (right) The addition of a two-storey extension in the seventeenth century.

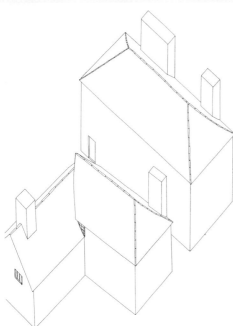

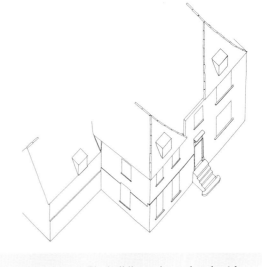

Figure 7.8d (above) The building as it stands today (also see figure 6.3), the amalgamation of the two separate buildings, probably carried out c. 1720.

Figure 7.8c (above) The construction of a free-standing house (c. 1680–1700) adjacent to the hall.

Figure 7.9 (right) Simple clues, such as different sizes of brick, breaks in the bond and building lines can reveal different phases of construction and provide clues about a building's development.

(Kind permission of Adam and Jill Singer. Drawing by Mike Dunn/BEAMS)

The building in question is unusual in appearance, but has the feel of a 1950s building (figure 7.10a). The timbers protruding through the masonry walls provide clues as to the building's origins, even though the remainder of the fabric appears contemporary with the estimated date of origin.

Documentary evidence, in this case an early twentieth-century photograph (figure 7.10b), reveals that the building was in fact originally an aisled barn and that the aisle fronting onto the road, has been removed with the existing building being contained in what was the central 'nave' of the barn.

Figures 7.10a and 7.10b (Kind permission of the Blewbury Local History Group)

To understand a building's development requires an appreciation of not only what remains, and has been added, but also what has been taken away. Determining what has been removed can be the extremely difficult, if not impossible, without some physical record or documentary evidence.

ALTERATIONS

Assessing what alterations have been carried out to a building, and trying to determine the reasons why they were made, is essential to gaining an overall understanding of the building's construction, plan and development, as well as its traditional and current performance. It is also an important part of the survey. It is not only the obvious physical alterations, such as the removal of walls or chimneys, that need to be taken into account; it is also necessary to understand alterations that have been made to the protective 'skin' of a building.

The alteration of the building may include what seem to be superficial changes, such as the removal of ornate pargetting to reveal a timber-frame, probably reflecting a statement of fashion or status, or a change in ownership.[6] This relatively subtle alteration, after the passing of many centuries, can have a profound effect on the performance and condition of the building. The removal of the render may have exposed timbers to the elements, and to conditions that they were not selected for at the time of construction.

Figure 7.11 Original rendering, with pargetting, has been removed and replaced with a cement render. The surviving remnants of the pargetting can inform how the building was presented and the opportunities that exist for reinstatement upon repair.

Figures 7.12a and 7.12b This building has been subjected to two fundamental changes; firstly the wall has been raised to accommodate changes to the roof. This has resulted in primary structural components, namely the wallplates, being cut and removed. Secondly, the photograph taken around the 1940s illustrates that the building was rendered. The removal of the render has exposed the timber frame to the elements, which along with poor detailing is causing problems of water penetration and decay.

Documentary evidence

Documentary evidence is often crucial to thoroughly understanding the history of development and alteration of a building. Physical evidence alone cannot always provide sufficient information upon which to make reasoned decisions. The combination of both physical and documentary evidence is ideal.

Documentary evidence can reveal (through photographs, sketches or written records such as previous reports, specifications or faculties for churches) the extent and nature of previous works, what alterations have been carried out, as well as the materials and methods used. This information adds considerably to the understanding of a building and the reasons why particular problems may be present.

Documentary information is not always readily available, and can take considerable time to research, but wherever possible resources should be allocated for this purpose. In the case of small cottages or town buildings, little information is likely to be gleaned that will be useful, but sometimes an old postcard or photograph, which can be found in local history books, can give a graphic illustration of the previous presentation and condition of the building, and what alterations have been made.

Case Study 7.2 Using documentary research

Figure 7.13a View of the church.

Figure 7.13b Detail of the walls removed of the protective rough-cast render and subject to subsequent repair with cement pointing.

The use of a combination of written and illustrative documentary evidence and physical evidence assisted greatly in revealing alterations made to a Grade I listed church in Oxfordshire and in justifying repairs recommended to address problems of damp.

The main alterations carried out to the church were undertaken within the programme of restoration in 1868. The nature of the works is described in a report describing the re-opening of the church and in an extract from *The Church Builder* in 1869. Identifying what was found and removed at the time of the restoration provided insight as to the type of materials that were present before the first major scheme of work took place at the church.

It was found that the church was rough-cast rendered, and that this was removed in 1868. The flint walls to the church have remained exposed ever since. Fragments of the render survived to the external elevations and this provided a clearer picture of the materials used and how the building used to look before the rough-cast was removed.

Since the restoration works in 1868 the church had been subjected to maintenance using materials that were not compatible with the performance of a traditional building. The use of impervious cement pointing externally, and modern paint finishes internally, resulted in moisture becoming trapped within the construction.

The combination of the documentary research and the physical evidence enabled the problems to be identified and a solution to be formulated. The protective coat of the building had been removed leaving the bedding mortar exposed to take the brunt of the elements. This had exposed the fabric to a massive increase in water penetration, exacerbated by the repair of the building using cement pointing (figure 7.13b).

Based upon historical precedent, recommendations were made that the church be provided with a rough-cast render. Irrespective of the evidence put forward the proposal to re-render the church was unacceptable to some members of the parish, as it would physically alter the appearance of the church they know and love. At the time of writing the causes of damp to the church remain. In these circumstances the best solution would be for the cement pointing to be replaced with a compatible lime putty mortar pointing, which would improve the performance but not drastically alter the existing appearance. This is the best compromise for the building.

If there is sound evidence for the existence of external rendering at the period of building then re-rendering in a suitable material may be justified on historical, visual and maintenance grounds. The wall construction of much church building in Britain, for instance, consists of dressed stone quoins, jambs and arches, and areas of random coursed or un-coursed stones which were rendered to keep walls weather-proof. The rendering may have failed and not been replaced, or it may have been deliberately stripped off and all the joints laboriously pointed in ignorance of the original design and intent or merely for visual preference.[7]

TYPE OF CONSTRUCTION

The surveyor must identify the building construction which has been used in the house or other property under inspection. They must be cognizant of the history of that type of construction and be aware of specific failures which can be found in similar properties.[8]

The materials and methods of the construction will dictate the performance of a building, the defects and problems that are likely to be encountered, and the repair options that will be available.

In many cases an understanding of the inherent characteristics of the construction can be achieved by means of a visual inspection. Measuring the thickness of walls will in most cases, combined with a process of elimination, provide a strong indication of the type and nature of construction. The presence of external rendering or cladding, and internal plasters or linings, will in many cases prevent the actual construction and condition of concealed fabric from being positively identified. Until investigative opening-up work is carried out no conclusions can be achieved.

Very few older buildings by the virtue of their age, will have escaped alteration or addition. A single building can easily incorporate several forms of construction, reflecting the materials available, affordable and desirable throughout its history. It is feasible for a building to have medieval timber frame origins, a seventeenth-century stone addition, a Georgian rendered façade, a Victorian solid-wall addition and a late twentieth-century cavity-wall extension. The number of construction styles that can be encountered in just a single building demands that the practitioner is conversant with a wide range of building types, the failures typical of each type of construction, as well as modern building methods and materials (see Case Study 2.2).

POTENTIAL PITFALLS

For those who inspect, survey and repair old buildings great care is required, because they can easily deceive the unwary as things are not always what they appear.

Figures 7.14a and 7.14b
The front elevation of a thatched cottage. What is the type of construction? The bond to the facing brickwork is a stretcher bond indicating that it is possibly a cavity wall. However, a closer inspection reveals that the front elevation is in fact mathematical tiles over a timber frame.

The load-bearing walls or structural frame of a building often display symptoms from which the surveyor will recognize and diagnose a defect. These symptoms may be clearly visible, as a crack in a brick wall, or be hidden, for example, by ivy, cladding or render. What, at first glance, appears to be brickwork may turn out to be mathematical tiles, and the rendered wall assumed to have been of brickwork may prove on closer examination to be of timber-framed construction, or another material such as shuttered clay or clay lump. The surveyor must therefore not accept things at face value.[9]

Knowledge of the detailing associated with particular forms of construction is indispensable to the practitioner in achieving a worthwhile survey.

The practitioner needs to be aware that the deception may be deliberate, as in scagliola columns and floors. Scagliola is a realistic but less expensive substitute for marble, made from a moulded and polished compound of basic plaster mixed with marble chips, appropriate pigments and other aggregates.

Figures 7.15a and 7.15b Inevitably, a method of construction will be encountered at some point for the first time. This relatively innocuous outbuilding on the site of a listed farm being developed for a residential development is constructed from a relatively rare form of shuttered flint walling, an early form of poured concrete. In these circumstances the characteristics of the construction and the detailing needs to be noted, and reference made either to text on the building type or someone with experience of that particular building type, before recommendations for repair or alteration are made.

Figures 7.16a, 7.16b and 7.16c In this case the configuration of the timber framing does not appear traditional, so further investigations have to be made to determine the type and nature of construction. The use of a hacksaw-blade between the joints revealed that the timber frame is merely nailed together and that the pegs are for cosmetic purposes. The pegs could be easily removed (figure 7.16c), whereas draw-bored pegs that are driven into bored holes in the timber draw and secure the timber joints together cannot be removed by hand. This simple assessment based upon an elementary understanding of timber-framed buildings confirmed that this building is not of a traditional construction, it has been 'cobbled' together.

In many cases the building type can be readily recognised. The structure illustrated above is obviously timber-framed. The key question here is whether the timber frame is of a traditional form of construction.

AIDS TO IDENTIFICATION

A simple means of assessing the likely construction is to look at other old buildings and boundary walls in the locality for clues as to the materials and methods of construction of the building being inspected, especially if it is of a vernacular construction.

Without knowledge of the detailing associated with the particular form of construction, which probably evolved over centuries, it is not possible to determine whether the building is suffering from problems associated with a break in tradition. Identifying the construction, and the detailing associated with it, is an essential part of understanding the whole of the building, and adopting a holistic approach. For example:

- the pitch of the roof and the overhang of a thatch
- the need for earth buildings to be built off stone underpinnings/plinths that are clear of the ground and a good protective overhang of the roof coverings
- The need for the sill beams (sole plates) of timber-framed buildings to be built off plinths that are clear of the ground

Figure 7.17 The use of pebbles in a boundary wall in a village in the Vale of York illustrates the likely construction of older buildings in this village and the immediate locality. Once identified, or anticipated, the type of construction will dictate the recommendations for repair as well as the suitability and likely success of available repair options. Invaluable clues as to the likely construction and detailing can also be gained where a building in the locality is in the process of being repaired.

Where the construction is not adequately identified it will inevitably result in remedial solutions that treat the symptoms and not the causes.

In most cases the inspection will be visual and non-destructive. In these circumstances the practitioner needs to know, for example, the expected location of concealed timbers (such as bressummers, lintels, bonding and fixing timbers) in order to make a worthwhile assessment of the condition and the likelihood of decay, and to produce a worthwhile report or specification.

UNDERSTANDING DEFECTS

Each building type suffers from particular inherent problems, a knowledge of these problems, and the available repair solutions is essential to a successful survey. Typical problems that can be encountered include:

Earth buildings

- bridging of the stone-underpinning course by external ground levels causing high levels of dampness to the earth walls
- slumping of earth walls, particularly near the base, where they are subjected to prolonged periods of dampness (see figure 5.3)
- poor projection of the roof, exposing the walls to weathering and accelerated deterioration
- rats burrowing and weakening the wall

Timber-framed buildings

- failure of joints
- alterations to the frame causing movement and distortion
- fungal decay and wood-boring insect infestation causing the failure of timbers (see also Appendix 3)

Georgian brick buildings

- snapped headers
- decay to lintels and bonding timbers
- poorly bonded rubble inner skins
- lack of, or limited, ties to structural walls
- use of patent renders of variable quality and performance
- removal of structural partitions

Victorian buildings

- separation of skins, snapped headers
- decayed beam ends bedded in masonry
- corrosion of ferrous cramps for masonry
- deterioration of terracotta facing materials

Figure 7.18a (above left) This rendered cottage has been treated as a masonry, brick or stone-walled building. A retrospective chemical damp-proof course has been injected into the wall. This is in fact a wychert building, a form of earth/cob structure in Buckinghamshire.

Figure 7.18b (above right) It is not good practice to inject a damp-proof course directly into an earth wall, it has little or no value and can actually cause physical damage. The damp-proof course has been inserted outside the Code of Practice of the BWPDA.[10]

Figure 7.18c (left) The symptoms of dampness have been treated not the causes, which are the high external ground levels that are bridging the stone plinth wall and the dense cement render that is trapping and displacing the moisture up the earth wall. The levels of dampness have softened the earth walling and could be putting the structural integrity of the wall at risk (see Case Studies 1.2 and 5.3).

An understanding of the building, and the defects likely to be encountered, will enable the practitioner to put the client on warning and appropriate repair solutions to be recommended. Without such an understanding the chances of misdiagnosis are significantly increased, for example the bulging in a Georgian wall that is a result of snapped headers could be incorrectly diagnosed as structural movement that is the result of a lack of lateral restraint. If the cause is not identified, and the structural works to improve the lateral restraint are carried out, the inherent weakness will remain. The wall continues to be at risk of failure until appropriate remedial works are carried out, for example by the use of stainless steel ties and resin bonding. There is even the possibility that the equilibrium of the wall could be disturbed by the unnecessary works to improve the lateral restraint, and as a result the wall will fail. A failure to understand a building and the likely defects that can be encountered in a particular building type can start a chain reaction of events that can result in, at best, unnecessary work, and at worst, structural failure.

PERFORMANCE CHARACTERISTICS OF MATERIALS

In assessing the performance characteristics of the building it is essential to determine the characteristics of the individual building components, as these will dictate the performance and the potential problems associated with alterations or changes to the traditional performance.

Stonework

Stonework is a widely used material in the construction of older buildings. Each type of stone has different characteristics, and in some stones the characteristics can vary considerably between individual beds where the stone was originally quarried. The vastly different performance characteristics of chalk and flint, two materials found in the same geological strata, is a good illustration of this.

Figure 7.19 Contrary to best intentions, the use of a hard and impervious cement pointing for repairing the soft chalk wall is accelerating the rate of deterioration.

Chalk (a limestone) is an extremely soft and porous building material that can be found in the same building as flint, which is a hard and impervious material. Chalk is particularly vulnerable to deterioration when exposed to the elements and is susceptible to damage and decay by a number of processes, the most important of which is exposure to water and salt. Chalk is a micro-porous stone and therefore wets readily but dries slowly. Chalk needs to breathe, otherwise moisture will be retained and this will lead to the accelerated deterioration of the building stone and also any timbers in contact with the walls of the building. In contrast flint is a hard, brittle and impervious material that is difficult to handle with vastly different performance characteristics to chalk. It is a common misconception that because the flint is hard a hard mortar has to be used. This can cause serious problems for a wall.[11]

The characteristics of each material therefore need to be assessed, with appropriate recommendations made. The best way to overcome the dilemma of deciding what is appropriate, is to look at how the building and others of its age and type were originally constructed and subsequently repaired and maintained. This will provide evidence, or at least clues, of what is appropriate for the particular building in question.

Timber

The age, type and quality of timber used in the construction or repair of a building will dictate performance in relation to its vulnerability to decay and its resistance to treatment. The type of timber will also determine the types of decay that can potentially attack the timbers.

It is difficult, and sometimes impossible, to identify the species of timber from a visual inspection, particularly where concealed by layers of paint. However, it is important to at least assess whether the timber is the sap or heartwood of a hard or softwood timber to enable a picture of the likely characteristics to be formulated. It is also important to identify how the timber was converted or cut for use in the building, for example is the timber boxed heart or halved as this can dictate the amount of sapwood present.

In practical terms, the sapwood of timbers has little resistance to attack from wood-rotting fungi, whereas in the case of the heartwood of timbers the natural durability and resistance to treatment with chemical preservatives varies with each different species. This can be well illustrated by examining two of the most commonly encountered timbers in historic timber-framed buildings; oak and elm. Because of their proven longevity it would be reasonable to expect that oak and elm would have very similar characteristics, but this is not the case. The Building Research Establishment (BRE) classifies the heartwood of European oak as being naturally very durable and extremely resistant to treatment with chemical

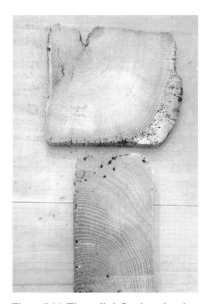

Figure 7.21a The typical grain characteristics of elm in the external slats to a barn.

Figure 7.20 The well-defined sap band to a section of oak timber. Note, particularly in the upper timber, that the wood-boring insect attack is confined to the outer band of sapwood and the heartwood is free of significant attack. The attack of the central heartwood in the lower section of timber may be attributable to the timber having being subjected to prolonged dampness and therefore providing the conditions for decay.

Figure 7.21b A typical section of oak has different grain characteristics to that of elm.

preservatives, whereas the heartwood of English elm is classified as being non-durable and moderately resistant to treatment.[12] Oak is denser and a harder timber than elm, and has a well-defined sap and heartwood; whereas elm is not as dense and has a poor definition between the sap and heartwood, it also can be prone to physically snapping.

The validity of the classifications used for the durability of timber needs to be taken in the context of the methods used. To assess a timber's durability, typically stakes of wood are driven into the soil and the time taken for the stake to rot is measured. However, this exercise contradicts the evidence of the continued performance over centuries of timbers that are currently classified as having poor durability:

> When we think of the large number of timber structures made of pine (*Pinus sylvestris*), dating back several hundred years, still standing in Scandinavia, it hardly seems relevant to characterise this species as being moderately to slightly durable in relation to fungal decay. This classification is, of course, correct if we sink the wood down into the soil. If pine heartwood is used sensibly, however, like the old master-builders did, the durability will improve greatly.[13]

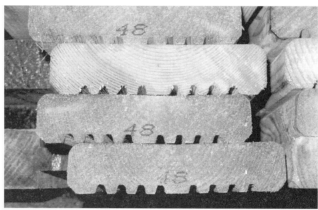

Figures 7.22a and 7.22b Pre-treated softwood timber being stored. Note the variation in the growth rings, some of which are very wide and are fast grown with a high percentage of sapwood. Fast grown timbers that contain a high percentage of sapwood rely upon chemical treatment to provide protection against fungal decay and insect attack. The success of pre-treatment is largely dependent on the ability of the timber to accept the chemicals. Where a timber has not been dried sufficiently it will be more difficult to treat. The variations in the penetration and therefore the effectiveness of the treatment of the softwood timbers are illustrated in the photographs. The careful selection and specification of timber, relying on the heartwood of good quality timber that is naturally durable would reduce the reliance for pre-treatment.

The key to longevity lies in the importance of good detailing, keeping the timbers free of the ground and prolonged dampness, and implementing regular and appropriate maintenance.

Understanding the performance characteristics of timber is important. For instance there is limited value in spraying the surface of the heartwood of oak with chemical pesticides to protect against wood-boring, as it is extremely resistant to treatment with chemical preservatives. This is often overlooked and treatments are recommended or specified irrespective of whether they are required or will be successful.[14]

> Another factor that needs to be taken into account is the compatibility of the materials used, for example, limestones and sandstones differ chemically and the interaction of the two can be a source of decay.[15]

The impact that the introduction of impervious materials can have on an old building has been illustrated. There are some other materials, not necessarily modern in origin, that can also cause problems for other components of the building, for example tannic acid from oak can have an adverse affect on metals, and the metals often need some form of protection, usually paint, against this potential agent of decay.

WORKMANSHIP AND CONSTRUCTIONAL DETAILING

It is often assumed that the workmanship in older buildings is of a high quality. However, many buildings still stand today with inherent defects that are the result of poor workmanship and detailing. For example, the accelerated deterioration of a single stone, where other stones of that type have been exposed to the same agents of decay, indicates the possible incorrect bedding of the stone. It is important for stone to be correctly bedded to suit its intended location on a building, to avoid accelerated deterioration and premature failure.

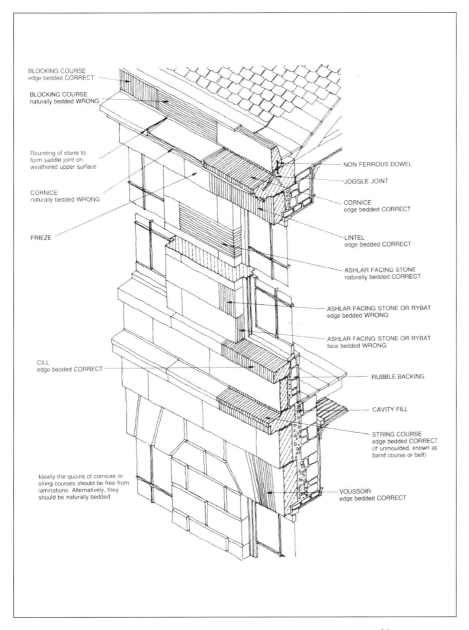

Figure 7.23 Bedding of stonework (kind permission of Elsevier Science Limited).[16]

Figures 7.24a and 7.24b These carved figures originate from 1849 when the church was built. Their varied condition illustrates the differences in the quality and weathering properties of the stone. It is the same type of stone, Caen stone from France, but the carved figures have each suffered from varying degrees of decay.

In this case much of the stonework was poorly selected, as it did not have good weathering qualities. These characteristics influenced the methods of consolidation and repair.

The quality of the materials selected to construct or repair a building may not have been apparent at the time they were incorporated into the building. However, time may reveal the true nature and quality of the materials used, highlighting those vulnerable to decay and accelerated deterioration.

MODERN MATERIALS

As the number of buildings recognised as having special architectural or historic interest expands, so the type and nature of materials of construction that need to be taken into consideration also increases. Protected buildings now include those constructed with technically innovative methods that are far removed from traditional forms of construction, such as the use of steel frames, reinforced concrete and even cavity walls (refer to Case Study 2.2).

In many cases, as a result of extension or alteration, there will be a combination of technologies in use, both traditional and modern. Therefore the inspecting practitioner needs to have an understanding of the characteristics of many forms of construction.

THE BUILDING UNDERSTOOD?

Probably one of the hardest decisions, particularly where finances are limited, is how far to go towards achieving a full understanding of the building. To determine this it is important to remember the objective of the survey or the extent of intended repair. Can the brief, the instructions of the client, be met with the information available?

Uncovering too much information that is then extremely difficult to collate and disseminate into a readily understood format, can create problems of its own. The practitioner has to somehow strike a balance. Perhaps the over-riding factor is determining whether reasoned and informed advice can be provided that will add value to the decision-making process, where the significance and value of the building is appreciated and understood, and will not be threatened by the recommendations of a survey or by proposals for repair or alteration.

References

1 Hall, I., 'First Analysis of the Historic Fabric', paper 2, module 7 – course notes, RICS Diploma in building conservation, The College of Estate Management, 1993, p. 1.

2 Clark, K., *Informed Conservation*, English Heritage, 2001, p. 15.

3 Feilden, B., *Conservation of Historic Buildings*, Butterworth-Heineman, Oxford, 2001, p. 185.

4 Department of the Environment/Department of National Heritage, *Planning Policy Guidance Note 15, Planning and the Historic Environment*, HMSO, London, 1994, Annex C.

5 Brereton, C., *Principles of Repair: The repair of historic buildings: advice on principles and methods*, English Heritage, 1991, p. 8.

6 Buxbaum, T., *Pargetting*, Shire Publications, Princes Risborough, 1999.

7 Ashurst, J., 'Methods of Repairing and Consolidating Stone Buildings', in Ashurst, J. and Dimes, F., *Conservation of Building and Decorative Stone*, Volume 2, Butterworth-Heinemann, London, 1990, p. 17.

8 Hollis, M., *Surveying Buildings*, RICS Books, London, 4th Edition, 2000.

9 Watt D. and Swallow, P., *Surveying Historic Buildings*, Donhead, Shaftesbury, 1996, p. 129.

10 *The Installation of Remedial Damp Proof Courses in Masonry Walls: Code of Practice*, British Wood Preserving and Damp-Proofing Association (BWPDA), January 1997, 6.2, Structural Considerations.

11 Lodge, D. and Wright, A., *Care and repair of flint walls*, Technical Pamphlet 16, The Society for the Protection of Ancient Buildings (SPAB), 2000.

12 'Timbers: their natural durability and resistance to preservative treatment', Cl/SfB (R8), DG 429, BRE, 1998.

13 Larsen, K. E. and Marstein, N., *Conservation of Historic Timber Structures – An Ecological Approach*, Butterworth-Heinemann, Oxford, 2000, p. 103.

14 Oxley, R., 'Is timber Treatment always necessary? An introduction for homeowners', SPAB Information Sheet 14. *SPAB News*, Vol 20 No. 4, 1999.

15 Clifton-Taylor, A. and Ireson, A.S., English Stone Building, London, 1994, p. 119.

16 Davey, A., Heath, B. Hodges, D., Ketchin, M. and Milne, R., *The Care and Conservation of Georgian Houses*, Butterworth-Heinemann, Oxford, 1995, p. 64.

DAMPNESS AND DECAY

8

A REAL OR PERCEIVED PROBLEM?

It is a common misconception that the two problems older buildings suffer from the most are dampness and timber decay. The issues surrounding dampness, rot, and wood-boring insect infestation generates irrational responses from those who survey buildings, and emotional responses from those who defend the actions of the remedial industry that has most to gain from the continuation of current perceptions. Unsurprisingly, those who own the buildings, or have the responsibility for repair, are confused. Whom should they trust?

Do they believe in what has become standard practice – in those who make a living from drilling and injecting chemicals into walls and spraying timbers with pesticides to kill insects? Or do they believe the minority that question the need for wholesale treatments and the use of standard solutions to treat highly individual buildings?

WHY IS THERE A PROBLEM?

It is the inherent characteristics of old buildings, together with the likelihood of past problems of fungal decay and wood-boring insect infestation, that make them vulnerable to unnecessary and uncontrolled damp and timber treatment.

The presence of a flight hole of a wood-boring insect can all too easily instigate inappropriate work, irrespective of whether the infestation is active or not. The same is true of readings indicating dampness on a moisture meter, which frequently trigger remedial action without positive diagnosis of the type of dampness found.

The problems of damp and types of timber defects that old buildings suffer from are often misunderstood, and the influence that the

Case Study 8.1 Treating the symptoms

Figure 8.1a

Figure 8.1b

In this case a cottage at the foot of the Chilterns has been subject to various programmes of modernisation, including a retrospective injected damp-proof course. A closer look at the building reveals that the physical insertion of the chemical damp-proof course caused damage to the wall, which is constructed in flint (figure 8.16).

It is evident that the damp-proof course was injected into the wall behind the render without positively identifying the type of construction.

The intended performance of the building and the influence of changes to that performance were obviously not understood. The use of cementitious renders and plastic-based masonry paint will seriously inhibit the ability of the building to 'breathe'. These repairs are inappropriate; they have adversely affected the intended performance of the building. Past attempts at treatment have been ignored; note the remains of an electro-osmotic damp-proof course

It is clear the causes of dampness have not been identified and eliminated before remedial works were installed. This has resulted in the treatment of the symptoms, which has caused damage to the fabric of the building. This Case Study illustrates that standard remedial treatments to a non-standard building, consisting in this case of timber framing, stonework, rendering and flintwork, are not effective.

introduction of incompatible impervious materials has upon the actual rate of deterioration is generally under-estimated. Serious problems can be caused by misdiagnosis and misunderstanding of the symptoms and by the reliance on standard methods of treatment. The resulting work in many cases causes more damage than centuries of decay.[1]

The remedial work carried out in the Case Study above falls outside the Code of Practice of the British Wood Preserving and Damp-proofing Association (BWPDA), a trade association for damp and timber contractors and surveyors.

The BWPDA Code of Practice lists the types of construction and materials that may present difficulties to the successful installation of a retrospective damp-proof course. This list mainly comprises types of construction that would be expected in traditional buildings, in particular those of a vernacular construction.

The surveyor should check that the property is suitable for treatment by a remedial damp-proof course installation technique. Most types of wall structure are amenable to treatment but the following may present difficulties which require special techniques to be adopted:

- wall of exceptional thickness (>600 mm)
- rubble filled walls
- stud walls
- walls of impermeable materials (e.g. flints, granite)
- walls bonded in irregular or very narrow mortar courses
- perforated or unusually bonded brickwork
- walls constructed of local materials (e.g. clay or chalk 'cob')[2]

A knowledge of the type and materials of construction is essential before making any recommendations. Unfortunately this is not necessarily put into practice, as illustrated in Case Study 8.1 and figures 7.18a and 7.18c. The types of construction and suitability for treatment were not assessed in accordance with the good practice promoted by the trade association.

THE PROBLEMS OF A STANDARD APPROACH

There are various forms of decay which commonly afflict the fabric of old buildings. Most of these can be attributed, in one way or another, to the presence of excessive dampness.[3]

The principal approach to treating the problems of damp and timber decay, promoted most commonly by the remedial treatment industry, is the use of chemical treatments. This is an over simplification but does reflect that chemical treatment has advanced at the expense of available alternatives. The exclusion of viable alternatives and the promotion of well-marketed products with guarantees creates a demand for these standardised solutions.

Traditional buildings do not lend themselves to standard solutions, as the problems found are very rarely simple or straightforward and this invariably results in the treatment of the symptoms rather than the causes.

Many buildings are subjected to repeated treatments, especially where they are regularly bought and sold. This raises fundamental questions about the effectiveness of the systems being used, the diagnostic skills of those who survey and specify the work, and the impact that treatment is having on the health of the buildings, the users of the buildings, and the environment.

THE INFLUENCE OF VESTED INTERESTS

The common use of standard phrases in surveys that make recommendations for inspections to be carried out, and subsequent reports obtained from specialist damp and timber treatment contractors, often seem to be a defensive response to the risks of accusations of professional negligence. It is, of course, good practice to recommend that further investigations be made, where the restrictions of the initial inspection or the limitations of the survey report, do not allow positive conclusions to be reached. However, this good practice is completely undermined as in many cases further investigations are being undertaken by 'specialist contractors', who not only have a vested financial interest in their own recommendations but will often be less qualified and experienced to comment than the practitioner who inspected the building in the first place.

The relinquishment of responsibility by the practitioner at this stage exposes the buildings to the pressure of vested financial interest, as damp and timber contractors are paid by the litre and the square metre to spray and inject chemicals, and to plaster walls with dense cement renders. They work in a sales-orientated environment, where profits are made primarily from the amount of chemicals and specialist plasters that they can sell. This is not conducive to providing impartial, informed and reasoned advice, so there is a risk that treatment may be recommended and carried out irrespective of whether it is required or not. This is contrary to the controlling legislation (the Control of Substances Hazardous to Health Regulations) and good practice guidance (such as the 'Remedial Timber Treatment in Buildings: A guide to good practice and the safe use of wood preservatives' produced by the Health and Safety Executive).[4]

> Before any measures are taken the problem should be analysed in order to identify the cause properly. In the first instance professional advice should be obtained, rather than that of a specialist contractor.[5]

The practitioner can overcome the problems of vested financial interest by making reasoned and informed decisions or by seeking the input of independent specialist advice. Currently, it will be difficult for practitioners to achieve either of these aims, because:

- the client or the system within which the practitioner operates will require instant solutions (see Chapter 2)
- the practitioner will not be confident in his or her own ability to make reasoned and informed decisions – a direct result of a lack of adequate training
- there are an insufficient number of independent specialists to turn to for advice that is free of vested financial interest

For the existing status quo to be broken there is a need for more practitioners to be ready to improve their knowledge of damp and timber decay. It is a sad reflection on the property professions that they do not have the skills to resolve one of the most fundamental problems faced by many older buildings, that of the misdiagnosis of dampness and timber decay.

DAMPNESS – WHAT IS IT?

To remove some of the myths and misconceptions that surround dampness it is worth examining what it is in closer detail. Dampness in a building could be classified as: an excess of moisture that is causing a problem; a cosmetic problem, the spoiling of decorations; the deterioration of the fabric; structural problems; or a condition that is having an adverse affect on the health of the occupants.

Figure 8.3 The removal of a cement render, which had entrapped moisture from defective roof coverings and rainwater disposal systems and thus exacerbated problems of penetrating dampness, revealed the original Roman cement render.

Figure 8.2 The problem of defective rainwater goods resulting in penetrating dampness and inevitably timber decay.

Figure 8.4 (left) A leak to this plumbing has caused rot to the floor timbers.

Where there is a problem of damp it usually means that the building is not working as intended. A damp-proof course has been bridged; there is a leaking downpipe; there is a design defect; or impervious materials have been used in the repair of a traditional building. A practitioner must have an awareness and understanding of the types of dampness. This is an essential requirement to successful diagnosis and making appropriate recommendations for remedial action. The types of dampness that can be suffered include the following:

Rising dampness
Rising dampness is the result of water being drawn up into porous masonry from wet ground by capillary action.[6]

Penetrating dampness
Water ingress through masonry above external ground level, is usually the result of faulty rainwater goods or roof coverings.

Lateral water penetration:
Dampness caused by water diffusing through the masonry directly from the ground, for example, when external ground levels are higher than the internal floors.

Trapped/displaced moisture
Where the evaporation of moisture is inhibited by the use of impervious materials, leading to a build-up of moisture and/or the displacement of moisture (and salts) to where it can readily evaporate.

Salt contamination and hygroscopic salts
Where moisture originates from the ground, salts will be carried in solution. These ground salts can include hygroscopic salts (chlorides and nitrates), which can absorb moisture from the surrounding environment, and can therefore contribute to problems of dampness. Efflorescent salts, usually sodium sulphate, are not hygroscopic but produce white crystalline deposits.

Condensation – surface and interstitial
Condensation is the process of a liquid forming from its vapour. When moist air is cooled below the dew point, water vapour will condense on cool surfaces as a liquid.

Other sources:
Defective plumbing or drainage.

How a building deals with moisture is important, and the sources of moisture have to be understood and identified. For example, the presence of 'moisture reservoirs', and how moisture is and can be managed, will dictate the problems that will be suffered, and the remedies available.

A typical problem of dampness encountered in older buildings occurs where the external ground levels have built up over the years and are higher than either the damp-proof course, if present, and/or the internal floor levels. This leads to lateral water penetration and is a significant source of damp to the building. This problem can lead to mould on the walls and fungal decay of the timbers in contact with the wall. It can also be easily misdiagnosed as rising dampness. The most appropriate remedy is for the ground levels to be reduced to remove the source of moisture and also create a 'moisture sink' by providing an exposed surface of wall where moisture can evaporate, which is particularly important for traditional buildings. Removing the source of damp, and improving the ability of the fabric to allow moisture to evaporate, will significantly improve the condition of the building and reduce the risks of serious fungal decay.

IS RISING DAMPNESS A PROBLEM?

Buildings constructed before the mid-nineteenth century will have been built without the benefit of a physical damp-proof course. In many cases this fact alone has been used to justify the insertion of a retrospective chemical damp-proof course. But the fact that a building does not have a damp-proof course is no reason to automatically assume that rising damp is a problem, or the sole cause of any problems of dampness.

> Rising dampness is usually not as extensive or as troublesome as other forms of dampness. In reality it is relatively uncommon, and can be easily misdiagnosed by surveyors.[8]

In many cases there is usually more than one cause of dampness to a building and it is therefore important that there is not a reliance upon single solutions to remedy a problem unless all the other possible causes have been eliminated:

> If a positive diagnosis of rising damp is being obscured by other faults the surveyor should recommend that the client remedies them first and then allows a period of time to elapse before further checks are made.[9]

Unfortunately this approach is rarely put into practice. Treatments for perceived problems of rising damp are carried out before any worthwhile assessments are made or sufficient time is allowed for the building to dry out. This is reflected in the number of retrospective damp-proof courses that are encountered. The level of unnecessary treatments reflects misdiagnosis, and a demand for single, instant solutions – which in many cases are trying to address problems that do not exist.

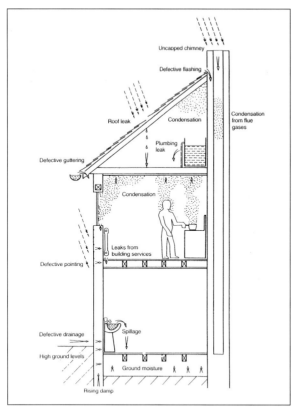

Figure 8.5a Examples of moisture sources and building defects.

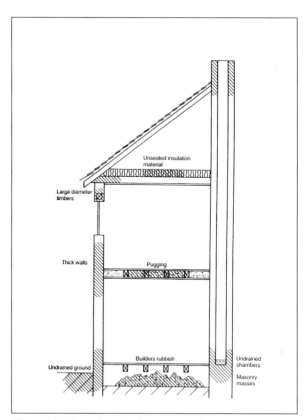

Figure 8.5b Examples of moisture reservoirs.

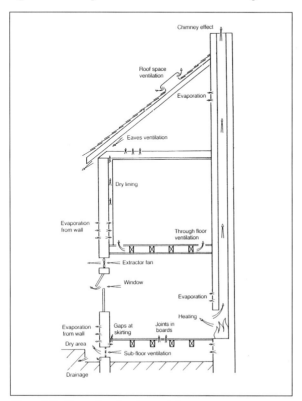

Figure 8.5c Examples of moisture sinks.

Figures 8.5a, 8.5b and 8.5c (Kind permission of Dr Jagjit Singh,
Building Mycology – Management of Decay and Health in Buildings)[7]

THE LIMITATIONS OF MOISTURE METERS

Moisture meters are used frequently in the survey of buildings without professionals being specifically trained as to their capabilities or their limitations. It is therefore important to understand the limitations of the standard electric moisture meter to avoid misdiagnosis:

- The moisture meter is intended and calibrated for use on timbers, not masonry.
- The percentage moisture meter readings in materials other than wood are not very meaningful.
- The temperature and relative humidity at the time of the inspection will strongly influence readings, and these can be highly variable.
- The moisture meter cannot differentiate between moisture originating from capillary action, either rising or penetrating dampness, or from the presence of salts.
- The readings are limited to surface readings (unless accessory equipment is used).
- The readings can be easily misinterpreted, as they can be affected by the presence of salts and/or past remedial treatments.[10]

Practitioners must exercise extreme care, particularly when interpreting moisture meter readings on non-wood materials. An over-reliance upon the results can lead to misdiagnosis and unnecessary work; for this reason the interpretation of the readings needs to be based upon an understanding of the limitations of the equipment and of what is actually being measured. It is unwise to recommend treatment where the assessment has relied solely upon the results of a moisture meter; it should be used only as a tool to aid diagnosis, not as the sole arbiter that it has unfortunately become.[11]

The moisture meter can however be used to provide information and aid diagnosis in a positive manner that builds up a picture of the problems being investigated. For example:

- Where no, or low, readings of dampness are found this can be a positive indication that the fabric is 'dry'.
- Where high readings are found this indicates a problem that requires further in-depth investigation.
- The moisture meter is calibrated to measure the wood moisture equivalent. This can be used to confirm the dampness of masonry by measuring the moisture content of timber in contact with the wall. This provides a more accurate picture of the level of dampness compared with relying solely on the moisture readings of masonry.
- Plotting the moisture profile and distribution across the whole of a wall or areas identified as being at risk in a building will assist in identifying the potential sources of dampness and any timbers at risk of decay.[12]

UNDERSTANDING THE SOLUTIONS AVAILABLE

As dampness is perceived to be a common problem in old buildings, assessing the range of available solutions is worthwhile, and an understanding of the limitations and strengths of the available repair solutions is essential.

Physical damp-proof course

In many instances this option is not appropriate in the repair of traditional buildings, as the masonry of the walls is rarely laid in regular or even courses. The successful installation of a physical damp-proof course is therefore either extremely difficult or impossible and can also cause problems of settlement.

Electro-osmosis

This is a system that relies upon electrodes inserted into holes drilled into the walls, which are wired to an earth. The electrodes are intended to provide an electrical charge that repels charged water molecules as they rise up the wall from the ground. Electrical charges in rising damp vary widely depending on the types of salt present. These salts may originate in the soil or they may be constituents of the masonry or mortar, and their presence and extent may vary according to their position along the wall. To be effective, an electro-osmotic current will have to be adjusted as appropriate along the wall to meet variations in the levels of dampness and salt contamination – this is usually impractical. Seasonal variations may result in the electro-osmotic electrical system being broken during dry periods and might not be re-established during the next damp period. This system, once common, is now rarely used.[13]

Figure 8.6 An example of a method of a retrospective physical damp-proof course comprising brick courses of replacement bricks of an engineering quality bedded in cement mortar.

Atmospheric siphons

This system comprises porous earthenware tubes inserted into holes in the wall. The tubes are intended to attract water to their evaporating surfaces by capillarity, drawing dampness from the inner damp surrounding masonry. The problems associated with this system are that the pores on the surface of the tubes become blocked as mineral salts accumulate during the evaporation process. There are also instances where tubes are set in cement mortar which counteracts the effectiveness of the tube system. This system has fallen out of favour and is no longer in common use.[14]

Chemical injection damp-proof courses

This is the most common system for the installation of a retrospective damp-proof course. The efficacy of a chemical injection system is dependent upon a number of factors and these include:

- the suitability of the wall for treatment
- the type of chemical used, whether solvent or water based
- the type of installation, whether a pressure-injection or gravity-fed system
- the methods of installation, whether it is mortar injection or chemical injected into the masonry

All of these factors combine to determine the chance of success and need to be assessed according to the conditions and circumstances found at the building.

A problem with chemical injection systems occurs when the chemical fluids do not entirely fill up the pores or completely push out the water in front of the advancing injection fluid. Instead, the fluid may tend to 'finger'

Figure 8.7 A building that has been subjected to both a chemical injection damp-proof course and the installation of siphon tubes. Note that the chemical damp-proof course has been injected into the bricks and not the mortar.

within the substrate, a process known as 'viscous fingering'. The fingers of the injected material form when the fluid takes the line of least resistance, such as via the larger pores and cracks. Ironically, the damper the wall the greater this fingering is likely to be, especially with solvent-based systems, since these are not miscible with the resistant moisture. Fingering is also increased by injection at high pressure. Reduction of the phenomenon can be achieved by low-pressure injection or by gravity diffusion of the damp-proof fluid.

Injection damp-proof courses are commonly installed into the brickwork, instead of into the mortar joints; but for a successful chemical injection damp-proof course the mortar courses must be well impregnated. This is because the only continuous pathway by which water can rise up and through a wall is via the mortar beds. For water to pass, say from brick to brick, it must still cross a mortar bed.

The chemicals in a chemical injection damp-proof course are only part of the 'system', as many rely on the use of cement-based plasters and renders to conceal and hold back residual dampness and salts from spoiling the decorations whilst the chemical injection 'sets', and starts to work in controlling the levels of rising dampness. The introduction of what are usually hard and impervious plasters into traditional buildings is contradictory to the intended performance. They can result in the moisture

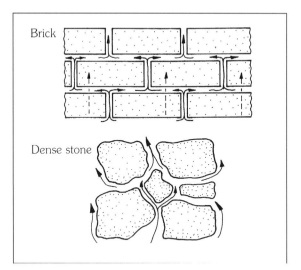

Figure 8.8a Moisture pathways.

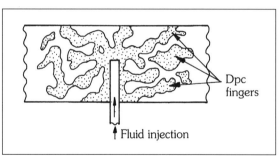

Figure 8.8b Viscous fingering of dpc fluid on injection.[15]

and salts becoming entrapped behind the plaster which causes them to be displaced to where they can readily evaporate. The chemical injection damp-proof course can at best only control rising dampness, so depending on the sources of moisture and environmental conditions, salts and dampness will eventually cause a breakdown of the plaster, or be displaced to previously unaffected plaster.

Where an effective injection damp-proof course can be achieved, the practitioner needs to be aware that it can concentrate moisture and therefore salts below this level and cause problems, especially in soft brick and stonework. This can lead to the accelerated deterioration of the masonry.

An understanding of the limitations of the remedial solutions enables reasoned decisions to be made concerning the appropriateness of a proposed treatment, and the likelihood of the system being effective. The constructional repair of the building, to remove causes of dampness and therefore decay, is a course of action that is strongly advocated by the British Building Research Establishment (BRE).[16] The use of retrospective damp-proof courses is in many instances a last resort where constructional solutions cannot achieve the desired aim.

So what is the best way of addressing problems of damp in an old building? As there are many potential causes, each must be carefully investigated and identified before arriving at any conclusions or making any recommendations. Effective measures can only be devised where causes are positively identified and eliminated, usually achieved with simple 'constructional' repairs such as: the clearing and realignment of rainwater gutters; the reduction of high external ground levels; the careful removal of impervious materials, and replacement and repair with traditional materials; and keeping plumbing and drainage in good order. Once the causes of dampness have been eliminated a period of time is required to assess whether these measures have been successful and to allow the building to dry out. This may take some time if it has been subjected to a defect for a number of years.

This approach is in accordance with good practice and the BWPDA Code of Practice, and is by definition a holistic approach. Unfortunately it is rarely put into practice, as readings of dampness lead more often than not to the knee-jerk reaction of inserting a damp-proof course, probably without first eliminating other potential causes of damp to the building, and almost definitely without allowing a period of time to assess if the works were successful or not. The practitioner must therefore guard against such an approach and ensure that the spirit of the BWPDA Code of Practice is adopted. This simple measure would undoubtedly significantly reduce the number of unnecessary damp-proof courses installed and dramatically increase the number of buildings where the causes of the problem and not the symptoms are treated.

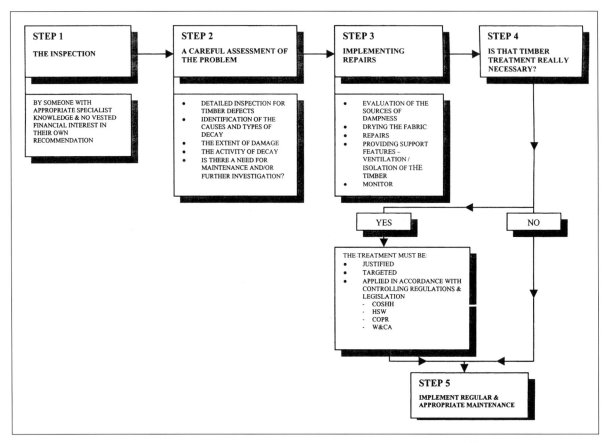

Figure 8.9 Is treatment always necessary? (Kind permission of SPAB)[18]

TIMBER DECAY

Decisions about what, if any, timber treatment is appropriate should be informed ones, based on a careful inspection and analysis of the building. Any inspection for timber decay in an old building must be carried out by someone who understands the types of construction likely to be encountered, the timbers used in construction, and the types of decay organisms that can attack the timbers. It is also important not to rely solely upon the advice of someone who has a vested financial interest in his or her own recommendations.[17]

To maximise the effectiveness of any attempts at addressing the problems of dampness and decay in old buildings it is important that a step-by-step approach is adopted, based upon reasoned and informed decisions, rather than applying standard solutions to highly individual and non-standard buildings.

If those concerned with historic buildings have more understanding of timber decay and more faith in their own judgement, then loss of historical materials can be minimized. Timber should only be exposed and removed if

Figure 8.10 Demolition of a wall reveals how it was constructed and the location and type of concealed timbers; in this case a concealed lintel.

there is good reason to suppose that significant decay may have occurred. This information may be obtained with a variety of techniques, but mostly from a close inspection of the building itself. The identification of faults that have allowed water penetration and an assessment of water distribution, together with a knowledge of the construction, will usually indicate timbers at risk.[19]

The vulnerability of timber to decay and its resistance to chemical treatment depends upon the quality and species of timber (see Chapter 7). If the practitioner has an understanding of the likely location and condition of concealed timbers and the quality, as well as the species of timber used in the construction, reasoned and informed assessments can be made, based upon a what is usually a severely limited inspection of only a small percentage of the actual building.

To avoid the unnecessary treatment with chemical preservatives it is essential that the inspecting surveyor can identify the following:

- The type of decay mechanisms most likely to be encountered, such as rot and wood-boring beetles (common furniture beetle (*Anobium punctatum*), death watch beetle (*Xestobium rufovillosum*), lyctus powder post beetle (*Lyctus brunneus*), and forest long horn beetle (family *Cerambycidae* – many species).
- Whether the decay is active.
- If the conditions necessary for continued activity are present.
- Whether it is of a type that requires treatment. For example, lyctus powder post and forest long horn beetle can only attack the sapwood for a relatively short period of time after the timber has been felled. In a building that is four centuries old these infestations will be inactive and will not require treatment.

Figure 8.11 Dry rot (*Serpula lacrymans*) fruit body.

Figure 8.12 This simple monitoring method of glueing paper over a timber perceived at being at risk reveals that death watch beetle is active, as new flight holes (circled) in the paper have been made by the insect during the emergence season in the spring and early summer.

Figure 8.13 Simple monitoring using timber dowels to determine the rate at which damp walls are drying out in a building that had been subjected to widespread dry rot. During repair works the walls were monitored to ensure that the constructional repair of the building is effective and that the risk of a serious outbreak of dry rot has been removed.

It is important to be aware that there is a significant difference in an attack by common furniture beetle and an attack by death watch beetle. In a recent case, a surveyor did not make a clear distinction between common furniture beetle and death watch beetle, only making a reference to woodworm (a generic term usually associated with common furniture beetle). In this case the surveyor was found to be negligent in failing to warn the client of the severe structural damage that death watch beetle is capable of causing, highlighting the importance of positively identifying the type of decay mechanisms and having an appreciation of the damage that it can cause.[20]

CHEMICAL PRESERVATIVES

The epithet 'preservative', although doubtless a powerful marketing device, is an unfortunate generic name to apply to biocides for use on timber, because it implies that decay will inevitably occur unless the timber is given some form of treatment. Yet timber is easily preserved in a dry environment.[21]

The fungi and insects that cause timber decay will usually only cause serious damage where there is damp. Chemical treatment alone will not address any problems of timber decay; at best it will merely treat the symptoms of a damp problem rather than the root cause. The extensive use of preservatives will not be required where the fabric can be successfully dried out and/or the timbers can be physically repaired.

The most appropriate and effective method of remedying timber decay is for constructional repairs to be implemented that will remove the sources of dampness. Often these need to be combined with the provision of support methods such as improving ventilation and/or isolating timbers from damp fabric. The removal of the conditions required for the development of a significant fungal and/or insect infestation, by the rapid, but controlled, drying out of the structure negates the need for extensive remedial treatment.

Chemical preservatives should be used only in a controlled and justified manner in accordance with the Health and Safety Executive's (HSE) and Building Research Establishment's (BRE) recommendations. That is, where a written justification can be provided, there is an active or a serious risk of attack, or the timbers will remain at serious risk as they are in contact with damp walls. Where chemical preservatives are used they need to be applied by trained and qualified operatives, in a targeted and controlled manner, in accordance with all mandatory legislative controls, codes of practice and manufacturers' recommendations.

It is possible that chemical treatments may have already been carried out, in which case, wherever possible the details of previous treatments should be obtained to ascertain the defects that were identified as requiring treatment and the chemicals used. The unnecessary treatment of timbers should be avoided on both environmental, health and legal grounds. Repeated treatments only increases the exposure of those who use and occupy buildings to different chemicals, which in some circumstances could pose a serious health risk.

One of the ways that the toxicity of chemicals is measured is by evaluating their lethal dose. A lethal dose is defined as the quantity of a chemical that would be required to kill fifty per cent of the population, and is usually assessed in relation to its effect on laboratory animals. These figures do not necessarily consider the risks that some chemicals may be carcinogenic or stimulate side effects in certain individuals.

> The general public has become much more aware of environmental issues through food scares, BSE, genetically modified foods and the abuse of anti-biotics and this has had a significant impact on consumption with supermarkets switching to organic foods. It is not clear why this public awareness has not yet switched to building materials and products such as these have just as big, if not bigger impact on our health and the environment.[22]

A more holistic approach to the use of chemicals is needed to reduce the potentially negative affects they can have, together with an improved understanding of the environmental impact and health implications of all materials and chemicals that are recommended for use.[23]

TIME TO TAKE RESPONSIBILITY

For more than ten years concerns over the use of chemicals have been raised.[24] Irrespective of these concerns and the development of an environmental approach to the problems of timber decay, there are still a significant number of buildings that are exposed to unjustified treatment. The actual consequences are unknown, chemicals are only withdrawn after problems or concerns have reached an unacceptable level – a cynic would argue when it has become politically or financially unacceptable rather than because of concerns over health.

It is important to appreciate that the use of chemicals for both damp and timber treatment is irreversible, once injected or sprayed the work cannot be undone. Carrying out chemical works creates a problem of disposal, not only for this but also future generations. The burning of treated timber, whether off-cuts burnt on site during the repair of the building, or disposed of in landfill sites, will potentially result in toxins being released into the environment at some stage. Treatments are often made without looking at the future consequences, it is assumed that the chemicals remain *in situ* and inert. This is not always the case. Chemicals

Figure 8.14 (above) This timber was attacked soon after it was incorporated into the building. The insects can only readily attack the sapwood, and have not caused any damage to the heartwood. The infestations have been dead for nearly four hundred years and do not require treatment. An assessment of the structural performance of the timber to determine if the attack has adversely affected its intended performance needs to be made and structural repairs carried out where necessary.

Figure 8.15 (above) This elm rafter has retained its bark and has only suffered from scattered infestation. This timber has not been attacked by wood-boring insects for at least a couple of centuries. It does not require treatment.

Figure 8.16 (right) This fruit body of a wet rot was exposed when weatherboarding was removed during repair. The cause of decay has been removed and the fungal decay is no longer active. The repair of the building will significantly reduce the risk of a new attack. The timber does not need treatment.

must therefore be used only as a result of carefully reasoned and informed decisions and in a targeted manner.

History shows that buildings can survive without treatment where there is adequate and appropriate repair and maintenance. History also shows that we can have too much faith in science, and the use of modern materials, without understanding the full implications of our actions until it is too late. We do not know how chemicals affect occupants or operatives, with some people being more sensitive to chemicals than others. There is a lack of reliable information available relating to cases of pesticide exposure and chemical sensitivity to be able to either condemn or condone the use of chemicals with confidence. This in itself is worrying – we simply do not know. It must surely be better therefore to veer on the side of caution.

The fundamental shift in attitude required by owners and occupiers to reduce the demand for treatment cannot be achieved without increased awareness of the inherent problems and an improvement in the education, training and diagnostic skills of property professionals, diminishing their over-reliance on specialist contractors.

Perhaps the simplest way of reducing the levels of chemicals used in the places that we live, work, play and worship in is to stop the treatment and re-treatment of infestations that have, in many cases, been long extinct.

The unacceptable level of unnecessary and damaging work that is being carried out under the banner of 'remedial treatment' shows that problems of damp and timber decay need to be rationalised and put into context, so that emotional responses can be replaced with reasoned and informed decisions. A holistic approach is required for any significant improvement to be made in how problems of dampness and decay, whether real or perceived, are addressed. This has to be the responsibility of those who survey and repair our buildings and not those with a vested financial interest in their own recommendations.

References

1   Oxley, R., 'Ignore It and It Will Go Away: The Problems of Uncontrolled and Unnecessary Remedial Damp and Timber Treatment in Historic Buildings', *RICS Building Conservation Journal*, No. 13, Winter 1995, pp. 9–12.

2   The British Wood Preserving and Damp-proofing Association (BWPDA), *Code of Practice; The Installation of Remedial Damp Proof Courses in Masonry Walls*, January 1997, 6.2 Structural Considerations, p. 6.

3   Thomas, R T., Williams, G. and Ashurst, N., *The Control of Damp in Old Buildings*, Technical Pamphlet 8, SPAB, 1992.

4   Health and Safety Executive, *Remedial Timber Treatment in Buildings: A guide to good practice and the safe use of wood preservatives*, HMSO, London, 1991.

5   Brereton, C., *The Repair of Historic Buildings: advice on principles and methods*, English Heritage, 1991, p. 30.

6   Building Research Establishment (BRE), *Good Repair Guide 5: Diagnosing the Causes of Dampness*, CI/SfB (L31), January 1997.

7   Singh, J. *Building Mycology – Management of Decay and Health in Buildings*, E & FN Spon, London, 1994, pp. 6, 7 and 8.

8   Oliver, A., *Dampness in Buildings*, Second Edition, revised by Douglas, J. and Stewart, J.S., Oxford 1997, p. 218.

9   The British Wood Preserving and Damp-proofing Association (BWPDA), *Code of Practice: The Installation of Remedial Damp Proof Courses in Masonry Walls*, January 1997, 6.3.4 Rising Damp, p. 7.

10 The British Wood Preserving and Damp-proofing Association (BWPDA), *The Use of Moisture Meters to Establish the Presence of Rising Damp*, DP1, November 1993.

11 Oxley, R., *Is Timber Treatment Always Necessary? An introduction for homeowners*, SPAB Information Sheet 14, Vol. 20, No. 4, 1999.

12 Oxley, R., 'Damp and Timber Treatment: Do's and Don'ts Guide 3', *RICS Building Conservation Journal*, No. 18, Winter 1997.

13 Oliver, A., *Dampness in Buildings*, Second Edition, revised by Douglas, J. and Stewart, J.S., Oxford 1997, pp. 198–9.

14 Ibid, p. 197.

15 Coleman, G., *Guide to Identification of Dampness in Buildings*, Wessex Publishing, 1990.

16 Berry, R. W., *Remedial Treatment of Wood Rot and Insect Attack in Buildings*. Building Research Establishment, 1994, p. 52.

17 Oxley, R., *Is Timber Treatment Always Necessary? An introduction for homeowners*, SPAB Information Sheet 14, Vol. 20, No. 4, 1999.

18 Ibid.

19 Ridout, B., *Timber Decay in Buildings: The conservation approach to treatment*, Spon Press, London, 2000, p. 188.

20 Murrells, P. Oswald v. Countrywide Surveyors, reported in *Structural Survey* Volume 12, Number 5 ('The Death Watch Beetle Case') and Number 6 ('Do Women Like Beetles?'), 1993/4.

21 Ridout, Brian, *Timber Decay in Buildings: The conservation approach to treatment*, Spon Press, London, 2000, p. xiii.

22 Woolley, T., and Kimmins, S., *Green Building Handbook, Volume 2: A guide to building products and their impact on the environment*, E & FN Spon, London, 2002, p. 4.

23 Curwell, S., Fox, B., Greenberg, M., and March, C., *Hazardous Building Materials: A guide to the selection of environmentally responsible alternatives*, Second Edition, Spon Press, London 2002.

24 London Hazards Centre Trust Limited, *Toxic Treatments: wood preservative hazards at work and in the home*, London Hazards Centre Trust Limited, 1989.

9 | SUMMARY – SUSTAINABLE SOLUTIONS

The manner in which traditional buildings are currently surveyed and repaired should be of grave concern to us all. The construction industry already makes unsustainable demands of this planet; if the mismanagement of the existing building stock is allowed to continue it will further add to the degradation of our environment. This generation has no choice, it has a duty of care to act to stop the depletion of finite resources and reverse the levels at which we now consume energy and pollute the atmosphere.

Changing the way traditional buildings are surveyed and repaired can make a positive contribution to the challenges we have to overcome. To achieve worthwhile gains this change will need to be approached in a holistic manner, one based on an understanding of the problems we face, the buildings themselves, the solutions available and an awareness of and responsibility for the long-term implications of our actions. It will require a significant move away from existing surveying practices and fundamental changes in the education and training of practitioners and craftsmen.

Current acceptance of what are damaging and self-perpetuating processes within the property sector needs to be challenged. That these processes are commonplace and therefore go unquestioned only serves to underline the extent of the problem, and demonstrates the general lack of awareness of the adverse impact that they can have – even amongst those who are already confronting the very issues discussed. We must now examine the manner of our practices and start again.

Perhaps the most effective way of initiating changes is for a code of practice to be produced that can guide property professionals towards adopting a sustainable approach to the survey and repair of buildings. Such a code could be based upon the following:

1. Respecting existing resources.

2. Understanding the building before acting:
   - Identifying and differentiating between traditional and modern buildings.
   - Identifying whether the building is formally protected.
   - Identifying the special interest and value of each building and its fabric, not only to this but also to future generations, irrespective of whether or not it is protected.
   - Assessing any changes in the intended performance of the building.
   - Determining the effect that any changes in the intended performance has had, or will have, on the condition of the building.
   - Wherever possible avoiding changing the intended performance of a building.

3. Providing a written justification of the need for any alterations or repairs to a building.

4. Devising repair solutions that are appropriate to each individual building; avoiding a reliance on standard solutions.

5. Avoiding reliance upon those with a vested financial interest in their own recommendations.

6. Adopting a respectful and conservation-minded approach to the building and its fabric. Wherever possible:
   - Maximising the retention of existing fabric.
   - Keeping intervention to a minimum.
   - Maximising reversibility of any interventions or repairs.

7. Ensuring that new materials are proven to be compatible with the performance of the building and have minimal environmental impact.

8. Advocating and promoting appropriate and routine maintenance.

9. Advocating and promoting good management of existing resources:
   - Reducing energy in use.
   - Minimising external pollution and environmental damage.
   - Reducing depletion of embodied energy and resources.
   - Minimising internal pollution and damage to health.

10. Informing your client of the benefits of and the need for a sustainable approach.

Adopting an approach based upon this, or a similar, code of practice would ensure that a more holistic approach will have been put into practice.

The survey currently acts as a catalyst for much inappropriate and damaging work. Its commonplace use, in its many guises, increases its influence on the condition of the existing building stock. Paradoxically it is its commonality that should also enable the survey to be used as a force for positive change, as it is integral to the many stages of a building's life, and is referred to by owners, purchasers, solicitors, financial institutions, insurers, builders, and suppliers. The survey can therefore be used to increase awareness, inform and empower; it can also act as an enabling instrument that can make the sustainable management of the existing building stock a reality.

To achieve worthwhile progress there is a need for a renaissance, a fundamental move away from tired and irrelevant practices. This will require property professionals to be prepared to adapt, so that they can meet the many challenges that lie ahead. They will have to learn to encompass the past, present and future requirements of each building – not just the condition at the time of the inspection.

There is a need for property professionals to rediscover traditional materials of construction and reconnect with traditional methods of repair. Increased awareness and understanding of these fundamental principles will generate greater demand for the skills and crafts required to repair our traditional buildings, which comprise one quarter of our existing building stock. Without increased knowledge and an improved skill base the problems identified will only worsen, and increase the environmental debt that the next generation will have to pay.

The building industry reaches into many walks of life, and we cannot separate ourselves from the built environment. This everyday contact and involvement underlines the important role that the built environment can play in achieving a sustainable future, and means we all have a responsibility to adopt a more conscious and conscientious approach to how it is managed.

The 'democratic intellect' of property professionals has been challenged; it is now time for the profession as a whole to start to provide a real-life service to the community. We each have a responsibility that we cannot neglect. Ultimately we have to learn to tread lightly on this earth if we are to act as good custodians. The extent and nature of the problems we face means that we must act to overcome present obstacles. We have no choice but to try and make a difference, and to adopt a sustainable approach to the survey and repair of a significant percentage of the existing building stock.

APPENDIX 1
THE RED BOOK

The RICS Appraisal and Valuation Standards:
published February 2003 and effective from 1 May 2003

UK Practice statement 3 Appendix 3.2 (RICS mortgage valuation specification)

Para 6.2.5 (Defects and disrepair): Where the valuer reports that work must be carried out to a property as a condition of any advance, and has also identified the property as being:

- of architectural or historic importance, or listed as such;
- in a conservation area; or
- of unusual construction

the Report must state that a person with appropriate specialist knowledge be asked to give advice on the appropriate works. In such cases valuers should only offer advice themselves if they are sure they are competent to give advice which, if adopted, would not be detrimental to the property's architectural or historic integrity, its future structural condition, or conservation of the building fabric.

The latest revision of the *Red Book* does not include the following background guidance that was included in its predecessor at Annex C to VGN 2A BN. This background guidance may be rewritten in the future as a Valuation Information Paper. The text that has not been included in the revision of the *Red Book* is:

Recommendation for works in respect of buildings of architectural or historic interest, in conservation areas, or of unusual construction

1   The process through which any building passes when used as security for a mortgage loan can easily lead to inappropriate works being undertaken. There are many opportunities for wrong decisions to be made:

a) First a defect must be noticed by the surveyor.
b) The cause of the defect may be diagnosed correctly or incorrectly by the Valuer.
c) The remedial treatment may be specified correctly or incorrectly by the Valuer.
d) The lending institution may interpret the Valuer's recommendations correctly or incorrectly when imposing conditions on a mortgage offer.

e) The building owner, his or her professional adviser, or builder may interpret those conditions correctly or incorrectly.

f) The work finally undertaken may or may not be executed properly.

2

For a fairly standard building type it seems likely that few problems will exist. But for a non-standard building there are many opportunities for something to go wrong. Damage can inadvertently be done to buildings of architectural or historic interest as a result of inappropriate advice and/or as a result of Borrowers, keen to fulfil obligations imposed by Lenders, usually on the advice of their Valuers, actin without independent specialist advice.

3

Given the complexity and/or individuality of the form of construction of most historic buildings it is usually not possible to be specific as to suitable working to deal with defects' without extensive investigation, which is beyond the scope of the Valuer's remit and/or competence. Many of the standard treatments used to overcome defects in relatively modern buildings can, when applied to historic buildings, cause considerable damage physically and/or to the integrity of the building as a structure of historic and/or architectural interest. Common problems include:

a) treatment for rising dampness;
b) treatment for penetrating dampness;
c) repointing or re-rendering;
d structural movement;
e) timber treatment;
f) windows.

Paragraphs 5–10 below provide notes on common problems and remedies in older buildings, including those of architectural or historic interest.

4

Having regard to the position described above, paragraph 3.10 of the Guidance Notes limits the advice which the Valuer should generally seek to provide in his or her mortgage inspection report [prior to revisions of 2003, now replaced by paragraph 6.2.5 reproduced at the beginning of this appendix].

5 Rising dampness

5.1 Old buildings are generally constructed of solid walls and these rely on their ability to lose moisture by evaporation to maintain reasonably dry conditions. Changes to the building such as coating with dense or impervious materials or changes in the vicinity, such as drainage or increased ground levels, can lead to increased dampness.

5.2 Standard treatments for solid walls suffering from rising dampness include chemical injection and the provision of dense renders internally. These can cause severe problems in cob, pise and clay lump walls where slumping can occur as a result. In flintwork the drilling associated with chemical injection can be very difficult and can cause severe disruption. In thick walls of stone rubble or rubble filled walls injected damp proofing is usually ineffective unless grouting is undertaken. Building constructed of soft stones such as lias or chalk block or of soft bricks can suffer severe decay of exposed masonry below an inserted damp proof course (d.p.c.) due to the concentration of dampness, salt deposition and frost action in this zone. Timber frame buildings also require special consideration to ensure that no timber is trapped below the level of any inserted d.p.c.

5.3 As has already been noted, dense renders inhibit evaporation of water from solid walls and are therefore likely to lead to increased levels of dampness in the wall material itself. Moisture entering the wall will be forced to rise higher until an equilibrium is established between absorption and evaporation. Further decay of the materials within the wall is likely and timbers within, or in contact with, the wall could become affected.

5.4 There are cases where stripping of internal plaster associated with damp proofing work has caused the damage or destruction of historically or artistically important wall paintings or painted decoration. Such decoration was common on walls and other surfaces, even in small cottages in many parts of the country.

6 Penetrating dampness

6.1 As discussed above solid walls constructed of porous material need to be able to lose moisture by evaporation. Frequently this process is interfered with by the use of dense plasters, renders and mortars or by the use of impervious paints and other coatings. This can lead to moisture becoming trapped within the wall, increasing decay of the building fabric, and deterioration of living conditions.

6.2 Standard solutions to damp penetration include the provision of dense renders, impervious coatings and silicon treatments. All of these could exacerbate the problem when used on an historic building.

7 Pointing and rendering

7.1 On historic buildings pointing and rendering is often condemned because it is a little crumbly or soft. As described above, the softness of a mortar or render can be an advantage and dense (cement rich) mixes can cause problems. For conservation work lime based mixes (often without the addition of cement) are generally used, and care is taken to match surviving mortars and joint types.

8 Structural movement

8.1 Structural deformation in historic buildings is often far more complex than in modern structures and misinterpretation is comparatively easy. Cracking is frequently attributed to differential settlement for which the standard solution is underpinning. Other common causes of deformation and cracking include unrestrained roof thrust, decay of bonding timbers, lintels or other built-in timbers. The cause of deformation in an old building may have been cured in the past (but this may not be apparent) or settlement may have occurred early in its life and may now have ceased.

8.2 A true understanding of movement in a complex building may only be possible following monitoring over a lengthy period. Underpinning of an historic building can also cause more problems than it solves and is regarded as a last resort. In some cases it may be better to live with minor structural deformation.

8.3 Specialist advice from a suitably qualified professional with experience in the repair of historic buildings is essential before embarking on major structural repairs relating to structural movement.

9 Timber treatment

9.1 The treatment of timbers against beetle attack and fungal decay is often recommended as a precautionary measure. Treatment companies will often require paint and other coatings to be stripped from timbers to enable treatment fluids to penetrate. If sand blasting is resorted to, timbers may end up looking very ragged. There is also a danger that painted decoration on timbers will be destroyed.

9.2 With current concern about the use of toxic chemicals for timber treatment it also seems unwise to recommend treatment unless active infestation is found. In cases where there is doubt it may be necessary to monitor timbers to determine whether an outbreak is still active.

9.3 In general, repairs to severely decayed timbers should be undertaken *in situ* as dismantling usually results in the loss of much more of the building fabric.

10 Windows

10.1 Unnecessary replacement of windows needs to be avoided as these contribute greatly to the character and integrity of an historic building. Timber windows are usually capable of repair and aluminium, pvc, and standard modern timber windows or joinery sections should be avoided on aesthetic grounds. Listed building consent may also be required for such work.

10.2 Old glass is irreplaceable and great care should be taken of it during window repairs.

10.3 Old leaded lights are capable of repair and can be releaded. Once again for reasons of integrity and appearance metal framed leaded lights, replicas with modern glass, and stick-on lead types should all be avoided.

APPENDIX 2
THE BLUE BOOK

5th Edition: European Valuation Standards 2003
Guidance Note 6: Valuation of Historical Properties

Guidance Note 6 covers the following matters: Importance of awareness of both the financial and cultural value of historic buildings; Recommendations for repair works or alterations; The subject of the valuation.

Introduction

GN6.01

Historic buildings are formally recognised across Europe as having a positive value, not only culturally but also economically – in terms of tourism, social status and commercial performance. Many historic buildings are provided with statutory or legal controls that protect the very qualities and characteristics that give them their architectural, cultural and historic value.

GN6.02

When providing advice, valuers need to be aware of both the financial and cultural value of historic buildings, the potentially negative consequences that their recommendations may have on the value, both financially and culturally, as well as the implications of any controls or protection. Valuers, when assessing their value, therefore need to identify and recognise historic buildings in the valuation process so that their financial, cultural, architectural and historic interest can be taken into account, along with any controls and protection, their condition, and the need for any repairs.

GN6.03

The valuation of historic buildings needs to be made in full knowledge of the special needs and requirements of these buildings, and these can only be derived from an understanding of the manner of:

  - Construction.
  - Performance (this expression relates primarily to the manner in which most historic/traditionally constructed buildings perform compared to modern buildings).
  - Appropriate, and inappropriate, methods of repair.
  - The extent and nature of any controls (legal and statutory).

GN6.04

Where recommendations for repair works or alterations are made within a valuation it is imperative that the valuer is confident that, if these works were adopted, they would not be detrimental to the building's architectural or historic integrity, its future structural condition or the conservation of the building fabric. Where any doubts exist as to the potential influence and consequences of any recommendations for works or alterations, the valuer needs to make a recommendation that further advice be sought from a suitably qualified person, who has no vested financial interest in any recommendations they may make and who has appropriate specialist knowledge in the repair and maintenance of historic buildings. Adopting this simple approach will ensure that the valuer does not make inappropriate and damaging recommendations that might erode the value of this finite and valuable resource.

The subject of the valuation

GN6.05
This Guidance Note concerns, inter alia, the valuation of historical properties. The term 'historical properties' includes properties *inter alia*:

i)   that are entered in a register of listed buildings;
ii) that are included in a historical buildings record;
iii) that are ones that, according to special legal provisions, are of particular importance to the cultural heritage.
iv) that are generally recognised as being of historical or cultural importance.

GN6.06
Once a property has been identified as belonging to this category, then the normal methods of valuation will be employed, but reflecting the material conditions and factors which apply to historic properties. Where there is any doubt as to whether or not the building being valued is historic, it is advisable for the valuer to make the assumption that the building is historic and protected by relevant legislation and controls. This assumption needs to be expressly stated within the valuation report, together with a recommendation that the assumptions that have been made should be confirmed by legal searches etc.

GN6.07
The elements that differentiate historical properties from others include:

i)   their increased legal protection; their architectural, historical, scientific or artistic value;
ii) limitations which have been placed on their enjoyment, their transfer, any changes in their use, and modernisation works,
iii) an obligation to make them accessible to society and for the purposes of science and education.

GN6.08
As part of the process of valuing historical properties, the valuer will need to consider the criteria he should adopt in deciding what is the appropriate valuation approach, method and technique, and should pay particular attention to:

any decisions of the authorities that have responsibility for the care and conservation of historical properties;
the provisions of local plans concerning the use of the historical property and its surroundings;
the purpose for which the valuation and the valuation report will be used;
the availability of market data and information;
the state of repair of the property to be valued; and
any other circumstances which pertain to the historical character of the property.

Reproduced by permission of the TEGoVA and the Estates Gazette.

APPENDIX 3
SURVEYING HISTORIC TIMBER-FRAMED BUILDINGS

An article by Richard Oxley, first published in RICS *Building Conservation Journal*, Winter/Spring 2000.

Introduction

Some of the oldest and most interesting buildings in Britain are timber-framed. The number of timber-frame buildings that survive illustrates that they are both resilient and adaptable, with many of these buildings continuing to be in active everyday use.

The majority of historic timber-framed buildings are listed and therefore statutorily protected. Some historic timber-frame buildings survive from as early as the 13th and 14th centuries and will have been subject to varying degrees of alteration, repair and decay. The longevity of historic timber-frame buildings means that they are usually highly individual and complex structures.

Timber-frame buildings are vulnerable to decay, particularly where impervious materials have been introduced. It is not unknown for the structural integrity of timber-framed buildings to be put at risk as a result of the introduction of impervious materials.

Unfortunately, the importance, complexity and vulnerability of historic timber-frame buildings is not always understood or taken into consideration when their condition is being assessed. This can lead to inappropriate recommendations that result in unnecessary, damaging and irreversible work.

Historic timber-framed buildings are special and deserve to be surveyed in a manner that befits their age and historical value. This article outlines the principal factors that need to be taken into consideration when providing a report on a timber-frame building.

Understanding the timber frame

1 Assessment of the timber frame

The timber frame is the primary structural component, the skeleton, of a timber-framed building. Consequently, it is imperative that the inspecting surveyor appreciates that the structural performance of the building is dependent upon the inter-relationship between the timbers and their joints.

This is often overlooked or underestimated, and it is not uncommon to encounter reports produced by surveyors and other professionals that do not assess the performance or the condition of the timber frame. In many cases the timber frame is inspected and reported upon as part of the roof, the walls and the floors, but not as the primary structural component of the building.

A survey that does not assess the performance and condition of the primary structural component of a building is a best misleading and in some cases will be negligent. It can therefore be argued that to achieve an understanding of the condition of a timber-framed building the frame and its joints need to be inspected and reported upon separately.

The assessment of a timber-frame will need to include:

- The identification of the frame type; e.g. box-frame, cruck, aisled.
- Noting the constructional detailing of the primary timbers and joints.
- Noting any alterations to the timber-frame.
- Determining if the structural performance of the frame has changed. The questions that can be asked include:
- Is the frame still performing as intended?;
- Are timbers missing, or have they been altered?;
- Have masonry walls superseded the structural role of the timber-frame? Is the building now a 'composite' structure? (for example, a combination of a timber-framed and masonry structure);
- Are the masonry walls capable of performing a structural function? A common problem encountered is where single skin brick infill panels take on a structural function where the sill beam (sole plate) has decayed away. In many cases the infill panels are not capable of performing a structural load-bearing role.
- Determining whether the joints are still capable of performing their intended function.
- Assessing the timber-frame as a three-dimensional structure, the relationship between the external and internal timbers.
- The identification of areas that have suffered from decay.
- The identification of past repairs and whether they have been successful.
- The identification of areas at risk, or suffering, from active decay.

2 Identifying the Timber

The age, type and quality of timber used in the construction or repair of a building will dictate its vulnerability to decay and its resistance to chemical treatment. The type of timber will also determine the performance characteristics of the timber frame and the types of decay that can attack the timbers.

Although it is difficult, and sometimes impossible, to identify the species of timber from a visual inspection every effort should be made to assess whether the timber is the sap or heartwood of a hard or softwood timber. It is also important to identify how the timber was converted (cut for use) in the building, for example, is the timber boxed heart or halved?

The sapwood of all timbers has little resistance for attack from wood-rotting fungi, whereas the natural durability and resistance to treatment with chemical preservatives of the heartwood of timbers varies with each different species. For example, two of the most common timbers in historic timber-framed buildings are oak and elm. The Building Research Establishment (BRE Digest 296, Timbers: Their Natural Durability and Resistance to Preservative Treatment) classifies the heartwood of oak as being a naturally durable timber that is extremely resistant to treatment with chemical preservatives, whereas the heartwood of elm is classified as being non-durable and moderately resistant to treatment.

3 Understanding the building's performance

It is important to appreciate how old buildings traditionally performed and how changes to the traditional 'breathing' performance can have a detrimental influence on their condition.

The introduction of impervious materials (such as modern paints, cement renders, fillets and patch repairs over joints etc.) will reduce the areas from where moisture can readily evaporate and increase the likelihood of moisture becoming trapped within the fabric and against the timbers.

Where the fabric and, in particular timbers, are subjected to prolonged dampness the conditions conducive for active fungal decay and wood-boring insect infestation will be present. It is therefore imperative that there is an appreciation that where impervious materials have been used to repair or maintain a timber-framed building that there is a strong risk that decay will be present.

4 Cladding and infill panels
The cladding and external finishes to timber-frame buildings are important as they play an integral part in the traditional performance of the building.

Answering the following questions will assist in understanding the traditional performance of the building, the condition of the timber-frame and the risks of decay:

- How was the building originally presented? (Was the timber-frame originally protected by rendering and/or limewash?)
- What alterations have been made? (Is the timber-frame now exposed when it was never intended to be?) (Has the historic cladding or finishes been removed or concealed?)
- What types of material have been used to repair and maintain the building? (Are they traditional porous and compatible materials, or are they modern hard and impervious materials?)

5 Assessment of decay
An inspection of the timbers most at risk, such as sill beams near ground level, timbers in contact with impervious materials and timbers below leaking roof coverings or rainwater goods, is an important part of the survey of a timber-framed building.

To appreciate the risks of decay to a timber-framed building, and to avoid the unnecessary treatment with chemical preservatives, it is essential that the inspecting surveyor can identify the principal agents of decay (fungal decay and wood-boring insect infestation). For example:

- The most common types of decay mechanisms, such as the wet rots and wood-boring beetles; common furniture beetle (Anobium puncatum), death watch beetle (Xestobium rufovillosum), lyctus powder post beetle (Lyctus brunneus), and forest long horn beetle;
- Whether the decay is active, and;
- Whether it is of a type that requires treatment. For example, lyctus powder post and forest longhorn beetle can only attack the sapwood for a relatively short period of time after the timber has been felled. In a building that is four centuries old these infestations will be inactive and do not require treatment.

There is a large difference in the significance of an attack by common furniture beetle and an attack by death watch beetle. In a recent case (Oswald v Countrywide Surveyors, reported in *Structural Survey* Volume 12, No. 5 'The Death Watch Beetle Case' & No. 6 'Do Women Like Beetles?'. 1993/4) a surveyor did not make a clear distinction between common furniture beetle and death watch beetle, making only a reference to woodworm (a generic term usually associated with common furniture beetle). In this case the surveyor was found to be negligent in failing to warn the client of the severe structural damage that death watch beetle is capable of causing. This case highlights the importance of positively identifying the decay mechanisms and having an appreciation of the damage that they can cause.

6 Assessing the rate of decay suffered by the timber frame
An appreciation of the rates of decay being suffered will assist in deciding what recommendations need to be made. For example, if the frame is suffering from accelerating rates of decay that are putting the structural integrity of the building at risk then works to remove the causes of decay and repair the frame will need to be implemented as soon as possible, whereas if the rates of decay are at an acceptable level and there are no structural issues a more sensitive approach can be adopted.

Carrying out the survey

The physical inspection of the timber frame of many buildings will be severely limited by the presence of masonry, renders, weatherboarding, plasters, internal floors and ceilings, as well as the contents of the building. In most cases it is difficult to determine the precise constructional detailing or condition of all of the timber frame.

The physical survey of timber-framed buildings is greatly assisted if a measures survey is available. The availability of such information makes it easier for the surveyor to understand the building, and to identify alterations and any timbers that are missing. However detailed information of this nature will not normally be available and the surveyor will have to collate as much information as possible on site. This is usually best achieved by sketching and annotating the timber frame.

To avoid becoming overawed at the number and complexity of timbers, the timber frame and the associated components of the building need to be broken down into achievable and manageable tasks. This can be achieved by inspecting the primary timbers first, starting with the cross-frames, gradually building up a picture of the timber frame until the secondary timbers (studs, rails and common rafters) can be inspected. From this inspection it will be possible to identify what timbers are present, what their condition is, and to form an overall impression of the condition of the frame.

The physical inspection of the timber frame will need to include:

- Selective probing with an implement such as a blunt screwdriver to test the resistance of the timbers so that an assessment of the extent of surface decay can be made.
- 'Sounding' the timbers with the handle of the screwdriver, or an implement that will not cause damage to the timbers, to gain an idea of the presence of decay below the surface.
- The use of a hacksaw blade, to test if tenons are present in joints.

None of these methods are 'scientific' or conclusive, but they are an important part of gaining an overall picture of the condition of the timbers.

Further investigations

The limitations of the inspection will in many cases dictate that parts of the building will require a more in-depth investigation so that the precise constructional detailing and condition can be determined. To avoid unnecessary work it is essential that any further investigations are not carried out by anyone with a vested financial interest in work following their own recommendations.

Further investigation might include careful and limited opening-up, such as the removal of areas of external cladding (render, weather-boarding etc). Obviously, this requires the permission of the owner, and in the circumstances of a pre-purchase survey will not usually be permitted.

Alternatively, not-destructive techniques can be used, such as micro-drilling, ultrasound scanning and heat sensitive photography. These systems do have limitations and are dependent upon the knowledge, skill and interpretation of the operative.

It is essential that any further investigations, whether it is based upon physical opening-up work or non-destructive systems, is based upon independent advice; a knowledge and understanding of timber-framed buildings; the causes of decay; and the decay mechanisms themselves.

Remedial work

Repair works, albeit well intentioned, can cause extensive and irreversible damage to both the timber-frame and the fabric and finishes of the building. The extent of damage caused by some repairs can be greater than that suffered by the building after centuries of 'gentle' decay.

Sensitive historic fabric, such as wattle and daub, earth and lime plasters and wall paintings, are all at risk where physical repair is required. Unfortunately many historic buildings have lost their historic finishes during programmes of repair. It is therefore essential that a greater emphasis is placed upon retaining these finishes and that stripping back to the skeleton is avoided at all costs.

An understanding of the types of repair options that are available, together with their advantages and disadvantages, is essential before recommending or specifying any repairs to a timber-framed building. The principal repair options that are available are traditional carpentry repairs; the use of metal straps, and resin repairs. Some of the factors that need to be taken into account when selecting a repair option include:

- Structural performance
- Consistency with the existing fabric and pervious repairs
- Compatibility; for example, the risks of tannic acid from oak on metal, and the introduction of impervious resins where there is a risk of moisture causing a problem of decay
- The level of intervention required to the historic fabric
- Practicality
- Cost
- Proven history of success
- Interpretation; is it an 'honest repair'
- Reversibility
- Aesthetics

The report

The information collated from the inspection needs to be reported to the client. The report needs to stress the importance and performance of the timber frame, which should be reflected in the frame being provided with a separate section in the report.

The report needs to provide positive recommendations on the condition of the timber frame, the type of defects identified, and where necessary the need for further investigations. The report would benefit from being supported with sketches and photograph that will assist in explaining the structure and any problems identified to the client.

Summary

Historic timber frame buildings differ from masonry structures. Those who inspect and report upon these buildings should adopt an approach that reflects the special characteristics of timber-framed buildings. This could be achieved by illustrating the following:

- That a conservation-minded approach has been adopted, that reflects the special architectural and historical value and importance of these buildings.
- An ability to put building conservation philosophy and knowledge into practice, thereby ensuring that the importance of the historic fabric is fully respected and that the building or its fabric will not be adversely affected by any recommendations made.
- An understanding of the protecting legislation and its implications.
- That each building is approached in a manner that reflects its individual nature.
- An understanding of how timber-framed buildings were traditionally constructed, repaired and maintained.
- That the timber-frame is the primary structural component, and that this is reflected in the manner that the building is inspected and reported upon.
- The age, type and quality of timber used.
- The importance of the traditional performance.
- The consequences of any detrimental changes in the traditional performance.
- The ability to recognise the type and nature of defects that the building is likely to suffer from.
- The available methods for appropriate and sympathetic repair.

Adopting an approach similar to that outlined above will increase the chances of historic timber-framed buildings receiving reasoned and informed advice, which will contribute to prolonging the life of these special buildings and their fabric, both the timber-frame and the historic finishes.

APPENDIX 4
HISTORICAL BUILDINGS PROSECUTION FINES NATIONAL DATABASE

With outline details where known. Deals with offences under S9 and S59 of the Planning [Listed Buildings and Conservation Areas] Act 1990 (or earlier equivalent) and the substantially increased penalties possible under the Planning and Compensation Act 1991. Levels of fine indicated below may be the exception not the rule. This table is not exhaustive – merely a brief guide to case outcomes where known. Compiled by Bob Kindred, Conservation Officer, Ipswich Borough Council and Institute of Historic Building Conservation National Council member. Details of additional cases would always be welcome and should be forwarded via e-mail to bob.kindred@ipswich.gov.uk

Fine [£]	Costs [£]	Works	Local Authority	Court	Date	Grade
200,000	13,000	Partial demolition, Stelvio House, Newport, Gwent. Owners McCarthy & Stone pleaded guilty to unauthorised alteration one day after building spot-listed. Judge concluded owners guilty of 'cynical commercial act'. Fine represented likely profit of redevelopment.	Newport CBC	C	1998	II
70,000	3,200	Total demolition of cottages, 46-48 London Road, Chatteris, Cambridgeshire. Owners fined £68,000 between them, and company £2,000. Fine based on the estimated value of the site after demolition.	Fenland DC	C	1989	II
40,550	32,145	Six S.9 offences and two S.59 offences, Somerford Hall, Stables and Gazebo, Brewood, S Staffs. Removal of features, replacement of materials, inappropriate repointing etc. Owner pleaded guilty. Ranges of fines for various offences £500 to £10,000.	S Staffordshire DC	M	2002	II* & II
25,000	5,402	Illegal cement rendering of C18 red brick elevations, Palace House, Newmarket. Fine stemmed from breaking an injunction to halt unauthorised work and Contempt of Court. Defendant – owner of property investment company – disappeared, fine and costs not yet paid.	Forest Heath DC	H	1991	I
20,000	4,000	Total demolition, 33 Union Street, Southwark, London. Owner fined £10,000 personally and £10,000 on behalf of his company. Appeal to Crown Court dismissed. Judge stated he would have increased fine if it had been within his power.	Southwark LBC	M	1999	II
20,000	2,000	Unauthorised alterations to The Manor Farmhouse, Lady Lane, Haydon Wick, Swindon. Demolition of two curtilage walls and breaching holes in the fabric of the building to insert extractor fans. Dudley Breweries pleaded guilty to four offences and fined £5,000 on each.	Swindon BC	M	1998	II

Fine [£]	Costs [£]	Works	Local Authority	Court	Date	Grade
18,000	5,158	Removal of attic floor, solid tread stair and timbers etc., Foxearth Hall, Braintree, Essex. Owner prosecuted on 10 counts. Pleaded guilty to all offences. Fined £2,000 on eight counts (maximum then allowed) and £1,000 on two counts.	Braintree DC	M	1990	II*
15,000	15,000	Substantial demolition, Dowles Manor, Dowles Rd, Bewdley, Hereford & Worcs. Building downgraded to Grade II after fire. LBC for extensive repair but extensively rebuilt instead. Owner took to Court of Appeal where fine was effectively halved.	Wyre Forest DC	C	1993	II*
15,000	577	Failure to comply with Listed Building Enforcement Notice, Crazy Bear PH, Stadhampton, Oxon. Unauthorised works to fireplace and chimney at public house. Enforcement Notice issued in 1997. Notice went to appeal. Works claimed to have been done before purchase. Landlord, J. Hunt pleaded guilty.	S.Oxfordshire DC	M	2000	II
14,000	10,000	Removal of c1731 interiors to convert first floor to flat, 67 Dean St, Soho. Developer and builder fined after pleading guilty to 7 charges of alterations without LBC. Benchmark case. Ignorance of listing no defence and contractor also held to be liable.	Westminster LBC	M	1989	II*
12,500	9,200	Unauthorised alteration and extension, 6 Theberton Street, Islington. Individual owner and company prosecuted for works to terraced house. Guilty plea entered but fines still substantial.	Islington LBC	M	2001	II
12,500	6,000	Partial demolition, Cressbrook Mill, Buxton, Derbyshire. Mill C18 built by Richard Arkwright. Consent for conversion work given but part demolition without consent. Developer pleaded guilty.	Peak District N Park	M	2001	II
12,000	25,490	Removal of 16th and 17th Century oak panelling and fireplaces, 162 Westgate, Wakefield. Mid-Yorkshire Chamber of Commerce pleaded guilty on two of eight charges. Fined £6,000 on each of counts. At time of discovery new owners had completely gutted the building.	Wakefield MDC	C	1997	II
11,000	365	Seven signs and lighting etc Liberty's Public House, 140 King Street, Great Yarmouth. Fined £1,500 on each of seven charges and £500 for unauthorised laser advertisement. Unsuccessful appeal to Crown Court resulting in award of further £300 costs to LPA.	Great Yarmouth BC	M	1995	II
10,000	3,000	Gutting of C19 house including removal of numerous features, 62 Kings Cross Rd, Islington, London. Removal of doors, fireplaces, ceiling mouldings all sash windows, chimney breasts and part of staircase etc. Owner fined. Described by magistrate as 'serious and flagrant' offence.	Islington LBC	M	1996	II

Fine [£]	Costs [£]	Works	Local Authority	Court	Date	Grade
10,000	1,750	Demolition of stack and all internal partition walls and floors, The Institute, Ramsbury, Wilts. Mitigation of poor state of repair not accepted. Developer fined. Failure to comply with S9(3) 1990 Act.	Kennet DC	M	1994	II
10.000	600	Unauthorised installation of shopfront prior to refusal of LBC, 35 Tavern Street, Ipswich. Owner, British Telecom pleaded guilty. Works inappropriate, crude and ill-proportioned. Corrected before trial, but Magistrates contended major retailer should have known better than to proceed.	Ipswich BC	M	2000	II
10,000	433	Unlawful total demolition of building, Love Green Farmhouse, Iver, Buckinghamshire. Work carried out by contractor under instruction from owner. Two offences fined £5,000 on each, reduced on appeal to the Crown Court to £8,320.	South Bucks DC	M	1994	II
10,000	+costs	Boots Chemists, Lerwick, Shetland. Contractor fined for removal of c1900 shopfront prior to LBC and PP being obtained. Architects DMWR had been told in pre-application discussions that shopfront must remain.	Shetland Islands C	S	1999	C
9,000	1,600	Unauthorised alterations to curtilage buildings, Golhill Farm, Edingley, Notts. Raising one section of roof, inserting rooflights, putting in domestic windows. Appeal to Crown Court dismissed. Magistrate found curtilage buildings to be protected and that prior consent should have been sought.	Newark & Sherwood DC	M	1997	II
7,500	574	Unauthorised internal alterations to Laurel Cottages, Totteridge Village, London. Developer pleaded guilty to 14 specimen charges for removal or replacement to windows and doors etc. Fined £500 on each of 13 counts and £1,000 on one count.	Barnet LBC	M	1998	II
6,500	1,500	Unauthorised alterations to exterior and interior, 2527 St Helen's Street, Ipswich. Seven counts of failing to comply with LB Enforcement Notices and Planning Enforcement Notices. Owner initially pleaded not guilty but changed plea on date of trial. Compliance by new owners. Reduced to £4,000 on appeal.	Ipswich BC	M	2000	II
6,000	30,000	Unauthorised removal of chimney stack, Thorpe Underwood Hall, Thorpe Underwood, York. Removal of stack (£4,000 fine) and consequent removal of chimney breast (£2,000). Chairman of Board of Governors of Queen Ethelburga's School fined.	Harrogate BC	M	2001	II★

Fine [£]	Costs [£]	Works	Local Authority	Court	Date	Grade
6,000	19,720	Unauthorised alterations to roof and interior, Carter Hall Farm, Eckington, Derbyshire. Removal of roof, plasterwork, architraves and skirtings from all walls, demolition of stud partitions and all except one door. Judge would have jailed defendant J. Power, has not he pleaded guilty and agreed to reinstate features.	NE Derbyshire DC	C	1997	II
6,000	12,000	Unlawful total demolition of building, 37 King Street, Royston. Owner fined £5,000; contractor £1,000. Councils costs £12,000. Total legal bill £30,000 approx. Defence that works were urgently necessary under S53[6] of 1971 Act dismissed.	North Herts DC	C	1986	II
6,000	8,000	Unauthorised alterations, Old Hall Farmhouse, Orsett, Essex. Both defendants, Teresa Gorman MP and her husband both fined equal amounts and equal costs. LPA also successful LB Enforcement Notices with 6 upheld, 6 given LBC but requiring ameliorating works.	Thurrock BC	M	1996	II
6,000	500	Unlawful demolition of C17 barn, Winterburn Barn, nr Lewes, Sussex. Owner was company with consent to convert to 2 dwellings. 2 Counts of £5,000 and £1,000, Appeal against sentence dismissed in Court of Appeal, Dec 1986.	Lewes DC	C	1986	II
5,250	200	Replaced all timber sash windows by uPVC, Farmhouse, Coates Lane, Downley, Bucks. Two years after enforcement action had failed to elicit reinstatement, double glazing firm fined £5,000. and owner, £250. Judge confirmed that a national company should have known better.	Wycombe DC	C	1992	II*
5,000	5,000	Failure to Comply with LBEN, Sandown House, Esher, Surrey. Appeal to High Court rejected despite vandalism prior to ownership. Appeal to House of Lords refused. High Court referred back to Magistrates for sentence. LPAs costs £11,000.	Elmbridge BC	M	1998	II
5,000	5,300	Unauthorised works to roof, and rear addition, 135 Stoke Newington Church St., Hackney. 3 offences against owner tried by Magistrates. Appeal to Crown Court: work to a flank wall, associated with roof, fine dropped but fine on rear extension doubled and award of Council's costs increased.	Hackney LBC	C	1994	II
5,000	4,000	Unlawful demolition of Collow Abbey Farmhouse, Legsby, Lincolnshire. Owners Mr and Mrs J Robinson failed to comply with condition on LBC requiring repair. Fines were £1,250 x 2 on two defendants in respect of two charges.	West Linsey DC	M	1992	II

Fine [£]	Costs [£]	Works	Local Authority	Court	Date	Grade
5,000	1,750	Unauthorised demolition of curtilage granary, Park Farm Cottages, Court Farm, Bramshaw, Hants. Within grounds of Grade II house acquired for renovation and in poor condition. Magistrates did not hold that condition was justification for failure to obtain prior consent.	New Forest DC	M	2002	curtilage
5,000	1,167	Unauthorised works to Grovefields Farmhouse, Hampton Lucy, Stratford-upon-Avon. Involved complete demolition of the main central chimney stack and unauthorised alterations. Owner who was also contractor was fined. Magistrates referred on to Crown Court.	Stratford-on-Avon DC	C	19/94	II
5,000	794	Removal of shopfront, 40 Chalcot Road, London N1.Failure to comply with enforcement notice issued 11 years before. Owner sentenced to jail for failing to pay but paid in cash upon being taken into custody.	Camden LBC	M	1984	not known
5,000	787	Unauthorised alterations Wig and Dickle PH, Long Stratton, Norfolk. Signs painted directly on to C17 brickwork. Building lessee fined, but work authorised by Managing Director of brewers, Innkeeper Group plc.	South Norfolk DC	M	1994	II
5,000	600	Unauthorised alterations Campions PH, Samlesbury, Lancashire. Addition of window boxes, trellis and canopy, Reval of window, replacement by door and extract duct to extension. Jennings Bros of Cumbria pleaded guilty.	South Ribble DC	M	1998	II
5,000	120	Removal of roof timbers in curtilage barn to listed farmhouse, Greet Farm Barn, Kirklington. Appeal to Crown Court 06/94. Fine reduced on Appeal to £1,000. Local authority costs reduced to nil on Appeal.	Newark & Sherwood DC	M	1994	II
5,000	+ costs	Removal of C18 wall in building, 14-20 North Bar Within, Beverley, Yorks. Defendant elected Crown Court hearing. Judge castigated owner for cavalier disregard of Section 55(1) of 1971 Act.	Beverley BC	C	1989	II
4,000	850	Unauthorised alterations to windows, Totteridge Green, Barnet, North London. Removal of two 1950s metal framed windows with new sash windows to three storey detached house. Owner pleaded guilty. Fine £2,000 for each window.	Barnet LBC	M	2000	II
4,000	750	Removal of mediaeval barn roof, Barn Restaurant, Chestfield, Kent. Defendants: surveyor and builder. Owner co-operated with Council throughout. Fine for alterations and part demolitions claimed to be essential repairs.	Canterbury CC	C	1990	II

Fine [£]	Costs [£]	Works	Local Authority	Court	Date	Grade
3,600	4,850	Unlawful total demolition of 10 High Street, Much Wenlock, Shropshire. Owner fined £1,800 Two contractors fined £1,200 and £600 each. Prosecutions brought under S80 Building Act 1984 and S9 1990 Act.	Bridgnorth DC	M	1995	II
3,500	17,500	Works affecting the character of Hainault Hall, Chigwell Row, Essex. Owner Mr M Sandhu, prosecuted on six counts including replacement of 6 sash windows, 10 internal window surrounds, 6 pairs of internal window shutters etc.	Epping Forest DC	C	1996	II
3,500	300	Unauthorised extensions and alterations, Langley Mill, Ascott-under-Wychwood. Defendant Mr Sykes, owner was successfully prosecuted.	West Oxfordshire DC	M	1995	II
3,250	2,500	Unauthorised alterations inc. opening up between buildings, 27-28 St Anne's Court, London W1. Removal of panelling (c.1710), removal of staircase opening up between buildings on 2nd and 3rd floors. Leaseholder pleaded guilty to 5 summonses fined £650 on each count. LB Enforcement Notice complied with.	Westminster CC	M	1996	II
3,250	100	Three sets of unauthorised alterations, 3 Westgate, Pickering, N Yorkshire. Internal alterations; holes in gable wall for flues; gable end window carried out late 1996. Owner advised to stop work 4-5 months before. Reduced on appeal to York Crown Court 06/97 to £1,500.	Rydale DC	M	1997	II
3,000	6,000	Destruction of redundant mill machinery, Burton Mill. Defendant was owner. Failure to comply with conditions to record under LBC before removal and reuse elsewhere.	East Staffordshire BC	M	1994	II
3,000	5,500	Partial demolition until only front wall remaining, 31 Doughty St, Camden. Architect and St Pancras Housing Association prosecuted on two counts of failing to comply with conditions and causing demolition. Architect fined £2,000. Housing Association. fined £1,000. Costs split 50:50.	Camden LBC	M	1993	II
3,000	3,000	Unauthorised extensions and alterations, West Close Farm, Combe, Oxon. Defendants Saxby & Burn, Owner was successfully prosecuted.	West Oxfordshire DC	M	1991	II
3,000	3,000	Unauthorised demolition of Braiton Messuage, Breacon, Belton, Lincolnshire. Building c.1750. Owner claimed poor repair. Initial not guilty plea changed to guilty in court on advice of Barrister. LPA considered building might have been repairable.	North Lincolnshire DC	M	2002	II

Fine [£]	Costs [£]	Works	Local Authority	Court	Date	Grade
3,000	2,150	Unauthorised sand-blasting of timbers, removal of widows and staircase etc. Hole Farm, Kelvedon. Remarkably unaltered mediaeval hall house. Some plea bargaining. Owner found guilty on 4 counts. Contractor Aquablast fined £1,000.	Braintree DC	M	2000	II*
3,000	2,000	Removal of plasterwork from three floors, 18 Holland Park, Kensington. House of 1862 with noted interior was to be converted back to a house from flats. Chartered Surveyor property developer fought trial on Legal Aid	Kensington LBC	M	1995	II
3,000	350	Unauthorised alts. from installation of beer chiller equipment, Old Bell Inn, Stoke Street, Ipswich. Damage to c1540 mediaeval doorway, timber framing and C19 doorway. Installer cautioned. Owners – Pubmaster plc fined on three counts of damage. Pleaded guilty.	Ipswich BC	M	1997	II
3,000	No costs	Failure to remove passenger lift, inserted shaft and ancillary accommodation, Orgreave Court. Failure to comply with Listed Building Enforcement Notice. Owner was successfully prosecuted.	Litchfield DC	M	1992	II
2,500	1,639	Unauthorised demolition of barn in unlisted conservation area. Defendants: Prew & Farmerson Ltd, Owner was successfully prosecuted.	West Oxfordshire DC	M	1990	
2,500	225	Unauthorised alterations, 16 North Park Rd, Kirby, Merseyside. Works , including imitation windows and uPVC guttering. Remedial works not done. Owner fined £2000 initially. Taken to court again on Oct/97, pleaded guilty and fined further £500 and £150 costs.	Knowsley MBC	M	1996	II
2,100	1,359	Failure to comply with Enforcement Notice, Kerry Avenue, Stanmore, Middlsex, in conservation area. Inappropriate render and window replacement on International Style detached house in conservation area. Owner and estranged wife separately fined and separate costs on each charge.	Harrow LBC	M	2001	unlisted
2,000	500	Demolition of cottage, Piccadilly Cottages, Enville, Staffordshire. Cottage in poor condition but also rebuilding of cart-shed/carport on it footprint. Defendant changed pleas to not guilty from guilty prior to trial.	South Staffs DC	M	1997	II
2,000	375	Removal of rare C18 Venetian window without LBC, Kings Arms Hotel, Bicester. Design Consultants prosecuted but not owners – Ind Coope plc. Only one other such window within the area was considered so important.	Cherwell DC	M	1995	II

Fine [£]	Costs [£]	Works	Local Authority	Court	Date	Grade
2,000	200	Failure to comply with Listed Building Enforcement Notices, 51-65 Wherstead Rd, Ipswich. Two of three fireplaces and C17 corner cupboard not reinstated replicated by new owner bound by LBEN. Despite mitigation plea, first offence and partial compliance, failure in extended compliance period.	Ipswich BC	M	2001	II
2,000	200	Failure to comply with condition on LBC, Old Smithy House, Dean St, Brewood, Staffs. Condition expressly forbidding inter alia use of power tools to rake out pointing ignored. Defendant leaded guilty and had billed the owner for works but had recovered less than 50%.	South Staffs DC	M	1996	II
2,000	+ costs	Removal of overmantle and fender from country house, Orchardleigh, Glos. Executor of estate prosecuted. Appealed at Bristol Crown Court where decision overturned. However, defining judgement on fixtures and fittings now in PPG15.	Mendip DC	M	1992	II
1,500	800	Replacement of timber windows with uPVC. George and Dragon PH, Wereham, Norfolk. Magistrates took into account that owner had removed offending windows by time of court action. Correct replacements in timber cost owner £3,400	Kings Lynn BC	M	1998	II
1,500	500	Replacement of shopfront on fringe of Town Centre, Ealing, London. Developer was successfully prosecuted. Enforcement Notice also upheld requiring facsimile of the original to be reinstated.	Ealing LB	M	1986	II
1,500	+ costs	Removal of working part of a mill without LBC, Apney Crucis Mill, Gloucestershire. Claimed plant had been stolen but later sold some of it. Company fined £1,000; individual £500. Owner also had cost of repurchasing and refixing machinery.	Cotswold DC	M	1987	II
1,450	840	Non compliance with Breach of Condition Notice, Homeleigh, Main St, Hoveringham, Notts. Also failure to comply with Requisition for Info. Council pointed to deliberate neglect of building. Defence pleaded financial mitigation which was taken into account. Fines £650 and £800.	Newark & Sherwood DC	M	1995	II
1,200	1,300	Unauthorised internal alterations to 2 barns. City Farm, Eynesham. Oxfordshire. Two staircases and two internal galleries inserted. Contractor fined.	West Oxon DC	M	1998	II

Fine [£]	Costs [£]	Works	Local Authority	Court	Date	Grade
1,000	45,000	Unauthorised alterations, The Old Rectory, Market Bosworth, Leicestershire. Protracted and expensive case where Listed status at the time of the offences was disputed. Owner fined on 2 charges. Required to rebuild costing £25,000. Owner's costs similar to Council's.	Hinckley BC	C	1992	II
1,000	1,125	Two timber sash windows replaced by uPVC, Regent Street, Barnsley. Chartered Surveyor owners, Smiths refused LBC to retain plastic windows. Further costs were uPVC windows: £600 and traditional reinstatements: £1,000.	Barnsley MBC	M	1991	II
1,000	+ costs	Demolition of C17 Dovecote, Northcott Court, Northchurch, Herts. Owner Peter Rost MP and wife, a Herts. County Councillor fined £500 each. Claimed dilapidation of structure and that actions were not deliberate.	Dacorum DC	M	1991	II
1,000	500	Unauthorised removal of internal panelling, 20 South Quay, Great Yarmouth. Followed refusal of Listed Building Consent to Great Yarmouth Port Authority. Timber panelling had been replaced by glazed screen and a first floor door renewed.	Great Yarmouth BC	M	1991	II*
1,000	235	Unauthorised demolition of barn in conservation area., Home Farm, Newton Blossomville, Bucks. Borough Councillor, pleaded guilty. Council's costs therefore low. Determined that the owners did not stand to benefit financially.	Milton Keynes BC	M	1995	II
1,000	250	Numerous external and internal unauthorised alterations. The Parsonage, Jolly Lane, Atlow, Derbyshire. Works despite prior site meeting with LPA. Remedial works cost owners £25,000. New purchaser couple prosecuted separately. All alterations treated as one case with one fine per person.	Derbyshire Dales DC	M	1996	II
1,000	50	Internal alterations, in conservation area, SuperDrug, Broad St, Ross-on-Wye, Hereford & Worcs. Internal wall removed prior to permission being given by the LPA. Owners fined.	S Herefordshire DC	M	1986	unlisted
1,000	50	Demolition of Lanrick House, Doune, Stirlingshire. On BAR Register since 1992. Owner claimed dangerous. Local authority criticised as inept. Scottish Civic Trust claimed fine tantamount to 'demolisher's charter'.	Stirlingshire C	SC	2003	B
650	250	Demolition of garage and store, The Manor House, Scotter, Lincs. Claimed ignorance and misunderstanding of the law. Owner fined £250; his company fined £400. Building within the curtilage of a Grade II Listed building.	West Linsey DC	M	1992	curtilage

Fine [£]	Costs [£]	Works	Local Authority	Court	Date	Grade
600	1,400	Unauthorised demolition of barn in conservation area., Chestnut Farm Stoke Goldington, Bucks. Consent to convert but owner totally demolished and rebuilt. Fine based on owner failing to notify LPA. Pleaded not guilty. Fine based on income of defendant.	Milton Keynes BC	M	1995	unlisted
500	5,000	Unauthorised alterations of lowering of cellar floor, 24 Castle Street, Farnham, Surrey. Owner and two builders pleaded guilty. Surveyor change plea to guilty on hearing evidence. Mitigation pleas for owner and surveyor resulted in conditional discharges. Builders were fined.	Waverley BC	M	1998	II
500	1,500	Demolition of east wing, Stillingfleet House, Stillingfleet, Yorkshire. LBC had been granted only for demolition of minor outbuildings and internal alterations. Owner fined. First prosecution by this LPA.	Selby DC	M	1994	II
500	500	Demolition of barn, Ivy House Farm, Odstone, Leicestershire. Owner claimed barn not listed and dangerous. Guilty on two charges, fined. Not required to rebuild. Council's costs of £2,150 only part awarded. Gain from sale of bricks ignored.	Hinckley BC	M	1991	II
500	350	Failure to comply with LBEN, 98 St Helens St, Ipswich. Original early C18 doorcase removed and replaced by crude modern example. Extended timescale not complied with. Second offence. (See Conditional Discharge below).	Ipswich BC	M	2001	II
500	300	Unauthorised alterations, 162 High Street, Ramsgate. New owner altered shape and materials of roof and replaced Kentish peg tiles and dormers with Velux rooflights. Fined for failure to comply with the Enforcement Notice.	Thanet DC	M	1997	II
500	250	Demolition of chimneys and cart lodge wings in conservation area. Rectory Farm, Bilsthorpe, Notts. Demolition was without Conservation Area Consent. Enforcement action ensured the chimneys were rebuilt.	Newark & Sherwood DC	M	1995	unlisted
500	N/A	Moving pair of redundant entrance gates, Heytesbury House, Wilts. Original fine of £10,000 by West Wilts Magistrates overturned by Swindon Crown Court. Moved in 1986 by DoT when estate severed by new A36 bypass. Pillars had been in temporary storage.	West Wiltshire DC	C	1995	II
500	N/A	Removal of statue of Icarus, Leighton Hall, Powys. Owner pleaded guilty but mitigating circumstances of removal to avoid theft. Statue separately Listed was valued at £50,000.	Montgomery DC	M	1992	II★

Fine [£]	Costs [£]	Works	Local Authority	Court	Date	Grade
500	No costs	Demolition and rebuilding, 10 Burlton Terrace, Bewdley, Hereford & Worcs. Works carried out without consent. LBC granted for refurbishment and extension. Builder who was also developer and owner was fined.	Wyre Forest DC	C	1986	II

MINOR FINES (>£500), COURT ACQUITTALS and DISCHARGES

Fine [£]	Costs [£]	Works	Local Authority	Court	Date	Grade
350	150	External alterations, 3-5 Mill Street, Bridgnorth. Defendant of no fixed abode subject of Committal Order for 30 days in default of payment of fine.	Bridgnorth DC	M	1992	II
280	50	Four Untidy Sites Notices, 152-156 High Street, Collingham, Notts. 3 Notices reduced on appeal to Crown Court from £70 to £30 each Fourth Notice – conditional discharge.	Newark & Sherwood DC	M	1994	unlisted
250	70	Unauthorised alterations, Rose Cottage, Thurgarton, Notts. Included concrete window lintels and uPVC rainwater goods. Mitigation plea accepted.	Newark & Sherwood DC	M	1993	II
200	614	Unauthorised signs, Harrods Stores, 7 Church St, Hingham, Norfolk. Followed Enforcement Notice and 2 warnings of prosecution. Guilty plea.	South Norfolk DC	M	1993	II
200	200	215A The Tuckies, Broseley. Because of defendant's personal circumstances, allowed to pay £20.00 per week.	Bridgnorth DC	M	1993	II
200	75	Unauthorised works. 72 Plains of Waterloo, Ramsgate. Painting the flank wall brickwork to an end of terrace house. Owners pleaded guilty.	Thanet DC	M	1997	II
200	50	Unauthorised works. Manor Farmhouse, Wellow, Notts. Unauthorised demolition and rebuilding of rear wing.	Newark & Sherwood DC	M	1990	II
100	250	Satellite Dish, Cricketers Arms PH, Silverless Street, Marlborough, Wilts. Owner prosecuted.	Kennet DC	M	1992	II
100	100	Unauthorised alterations prior to retrospective LBC application (refused), 30 Albion Place, Northampton. Rendered over rear elevation brickwork and reduction of chimney stack on early C19 residential premises.	Northampton BC	M	1996	II
CD	45,500	Twenty-two offences, five guilty pleas of unauthorised alterations, Stream Farm, Iden Green, Kent. Judicial Review lost but charges dropped when LA's costs met. Defendant's estimated costs £50,000	Tunbridge Wells BC	M	20/02	II
CD	100	Failure to reinstate 3 sliding sash windows, 98 St Helens St, Ipswich. Defendant given conditional discharge because of financial circumstances. but still required to reinstate.	Ipswich BC	M	1994	II

CD	50	Unauthorised alterations at The Granary, Ulting Hall, Ulting, Maldon, Essex. Works included insertion of windows and brick plinth, interior plasterboard, brick nogging between studs etc.	Maldon DC	M	1997	II
CD		Numerous internal alterations/destruction of fabric, 3 High Street, Debenham, Suffolk. Owner absolute discharge, builder conditional discharge with costs awarded against builder.	Mid Suffolk DC	M	1997	II*
AD		Installation of solid shopfront roller shutter, Bridwell Alley, Norwich. Defendant a TV personality targeted by animal rights activists. Separate Enforcement Notice upheld.	Norwich CC	M	1991	II
AD		Removal of fireplace at The Knowle, Eardington. Defendant given absolute discharge because he was bankrupt.	Bridgnorth DC	M	1995	II
AD		Demolition of leucomb, Uppey House, Church St, Uppey, Weymouth. No financial benefit accrued from works. Owners required to reinstate. Loss of EH grant greater than maximum fine.	Weymouth BC	M	1995	II

Fine [£]	Costs [£]	Works	Local Authority	Court	Date	Grade
AD		Unauthorised alterations, 137 Talgarth Rd, London W14. LPA took 4 charges as 1 offence. Only 3 proved, one not proved so case dismissed.	Hammersmith & Fulham LB	M	2001	II

CUSTODIAL SENTENCES

Sentence	Work	Court	Date	Grade
12 months +	Attempt to defraud – theft of fireplaces Rangemore Hall, East Staffordshire [Grade II*]. 3 owners made fraudulent claim of theft. Fireplaces sold to Ireland antique dealer. Police prosecution under Fraud Act. LB Enforcement Notices also served. 2 pleaded guilty, one not guilty. One given 12 months and two given 9 months.	Crown Court	2000	II
8 months +	Theft of lead from roof, Revesby Abbey, Lincolnshire [Grade I]. Building in the control of English Heritage. Three defendants sentenced to 8 months, 6 months, and 100 hrs. community service respectively.	Lincoln Crown Court	1989	I
4 months +	Attempt to expedite demolition by explosives, Methodist Chapel, Dartmouth. Owner persuaded contractor to use explosives to damage sufficient to justify demolition. Owner sentenced to 4 months; operative given 4 months with 3 months suspended for two years.	Magistrates Court	1992	II

| Until fine paid | Failure to comply with 1984 enforcement notice, 40 Chalcot Rd, Camden, (*See also schedule of fines above*). Persistent prevarication over long period, frustrating the implementation of the Planning legislation. Court sentenced the defendant to be jailed until fine paid. Fine paid day before defendant's imprisonment. | Magistrates Court | 1984 | not known |

Notes

Fines   AD = Absolute discharge; CD = Conditional discharge *= reduced to £4,000 on Appeal

Court   M = Magistrates Court; S = Sheriffs Court [Scotland]; C = Crown Court; H = High Court; CA = Court of Appeal

COMPARISON FINES UNDER PLANNING LEGISLATION

Fine [£]	Costs [£]	Works	Local Authority	Court	Date
30,000		Felling of three TPO trees			
25,000		Breach of Enforcement Notice. Building stable block contrary to gen. planning policy and intrusion into open countryside. Judge intended fine to act as deterrent.	Taunton BC	C	1994
6,400		6 Enforcement Notices since 1988. Mobile home in green belt without Planning Permission. Appellant 'led LA a merry dance over the years'.	Dartford BC	C	1994
3,000	1,000	Felling of a TPO tree, Reduced from £6,000 on appeal.		C	1989

SOME COMPARISON FINES UNDER ANCIENT MONUMENTS LEGISLATION

Fine [£]	Works	Court	Date
15,000	Works of underpinning to warehouse which damaged underground remains of Winchester Palace, London. Fine reduced in Court of Appeal from £75,000 with £1,000 on the basis that work stopped immediately; guilty plea entered and fine would have been 75% of annual company profits.	CA	1992
15,000	Excavations around Binchester Hall hotel damaging Roman fort and settlement. Owner pleaded guilty to 3 counts. On basis of negligence not deliberate damage, fine reduced in Court of Appeal from £33,000 but award of costs of £10,000 against defendant were not reduced.	CA	1991
15,000	Creating an artificial lake on the site of Legbourne Priory, a scheduled mediaeval nunnery, Louth, Lincolnshire. Visible earthworks under pasture until 1988. Consent not south as unlikely to be granted. Owner pleaded guilty and undertook to restore. Judge Hutchinson, Lincoln Crown Court 'a bad offence of its kind'.		1990
3,000	Ploughing of Roman town of Alcester scheduled site. Fine reduced in Court of Appeal from £10,000 with £4,914 on the basis that it was not deliberate but due to a misunderstanding.	CA	1988

Reproduced by kind permission of Bob Kindred.

APPENDIX 5
ENGLISH HERITAGE – PRINCIPLES OF REPAIR

1 Introduction

The purpose of this volume is to provide guidance to building owners and their professional advisers on the principles which should be applied in the repair of historic buildings and monuments and on the methods which are appropriate to the observance of those principles.

The book has been prepared in order to satisfy a long-standing demand for such guidance from English Heritage and with the aim of achieving a consistency of approach in historic building repairs.

The basic principles and objectives which are relevant to an individual case should be established at the outset and should then be applied to generate solutions to particular problems and specific methods for repair.

It is essential to identify causes before specifying remedies and in pursuit of this there is a need for a careful and accurate diagnosis including, where appropriate, monitoring of the structure.

The recommendations on methods of repair are intended for guidance only and should be considered in the context of a careful analysis of the needs of a particular building. There can be no standard specification for the repair of historic buildings and monuments.

It is important to continue to look at a building as work proceeds in case the nature of some of the repairs is found to change with the result that methods may need to be revised.

Perhaps most important of all are the attitudes and degree of sensitivity of building owners and their professional advisers.

2 Principles of repair

2.1 The purpose of repair
The primary purpose of repair is to restrain the process of decay without damaging the character of buildings or monuments, altering the features which give them their historic or architectural importance, or unnecessarily disturbing or destroying historic fabric.

2.2 The need for repair
Works of repair must be kept to the minimum required to stabilise and conserve buildings and monuments, with the aim of achieving a sufficiently sound structural condition to ensure their long-term survival.

2.3 Avoiding unnecessary damage
The authenticity of a historic building or monument depends most crucially on integrity of its fabric and on its design, which may be original or may incorporate different periods of addition and alteration. The unnecessary replacement of historic fabric, no matter how carefully the work is carried out, will have an

adverse effect on the appearance of a building or monument, will seriously diminish its authenticity, and will significantly reduce its value as a source of historical information. Inevitably elements of the fabric will decay, or become defective in other ways, but the rate and extent to which this occurs will vary. For example, certain types of roof covering and protective wall covering will require periodic complete or major replacement. Other elements, in particular masonry and the framing of walls and roofs, are more likely to decay slowly and in parts, rather than comprehensively, and require a more selective approach.

2.4 Analysing historic development
A thorough understanding of the historical development of a building or monument is a necessary preliminary to its repair. This may involve archaeological and architectural investigation, documentary research, recording and interpretation of the particular structure, and its assessment in a wider historic context may be required. Such processes may, when appropriate, need to continue during the course of repairs. Satisfactory arrangements should be made for the subsequent preservation of all records.

2.5 Analysing the causes of defects
In addition to an analysis of the historical development of the building or monument, the detailed design of repairs should also be preceded by the long-term observation of its structural defects, together with an investigation of the nature and condition of its materials and of the causes, processes, and rates of decay. To repair or replace decayed fabric without first carrying out such an investigation is to invite the repetition of problems.

2.6 Adopting proven techniques
Repair techniques should match or be compatible with existing materials and methods of construction, in order to preserve the appearance and historic integrity of the building or monument, and to ensure that the work has an appropriate life. Exceptions should only be considered where the existing fabric has failed because of inherent defects of design or incorrect specification of materials, rather than from neglect of maintenance or because it has completed its expected life. New methods and techniques should only be used where they have proved themselves over a sufficient period, and where traditional alternatives cannot be identified. In deciding whether to adopt new methods and techniques it will be necessary to balance the benefit to the building or monument in the future against any damage which may be caused to its appearance or historic integrity.

2.7 Truth to materials
Repairs should be executed honestly, with no attempt at disguise or artificial ageing, but should not be unnecessarily obtrusive or unsympathetic in appearance. When the replacement of historic fabric is unavoidably extensive, or significant in other ways, the work may be discreetly dated for future reference.

2.8 Removal of later alterations
Additions or alterations, including earlier repairs, are of importance for the part they play in the cumulative history of a building or monument. There will always be a strong presumption in favour of their retention. Whilst a programme of repairs may offer the opportunity for removing, after recording, features which are of no intrinsic value in themselves, and which seriously disrupt the overall

architectural interest and aesthetic value of the building or monument, the full implications of doing so must be carefully considered in advance, and potential architectural and aesthetic gains must be balanced against the loss of historic integrity.

2.9 Restoration of lost features

Some elements of a building or monument which are important to its design, for example balustrades, pinnacles, cornices, hoodmoulds, window tracery, and members of a timber frame or roof truss, may have been lost in the past. Where these are of structural significance, they will be put back in the course of repair; but a programme of repair may also offer the opportunity for reinstatement of missing non-structural elements, provided that sufficient evidence exists for accurate replacement, no loss of historic fabric occurs, and the necessary statutory consents are obtained in advance. Speculative reconstruction is always unjustified.

2.10 Safeguarding the future

An historic building or monument should be regularly monitored and maintained, and, wherever possible, provided with an appropriate and sympathetic use. This is the best way of securing its future, and of keeping further repair requirements to a minimum.

FURTHER READING

Ashurst, John and Nichola, Practical Building Conservation Series, English Heritage Technical Handbooks, Gower Technical Press, Aldershot 1988.

    Volume 1   *Stone Masonry*
    Volume 2   *Brick, Terracotta and Earth*
    Volume 3   *Mortars, Plasters and Renders*
    Volume 4   *Metals*
    Volume 5   *Wood, Glass and Resins*

Bordass, W. and Bemrose, C., *Heating Your Church*, Council for the Care of Churches, Church House Publishing, London, 1996.

Borer, P. and Harris, C., *The Whole House Book – Ecological Building Design and Materials*, The Centre for Alternative Technology Publications, 1998.

Bravery, A.F., Berry, R.W., Carey, J.K., and Cooper, D.E., *Recognising Wood Rot and Insect Damage in Buildings*, Building Research Establishment, 1992.

Brereton, C., *The Repair of Historic Buildings: Advice on principles and methods*, English Heritage, London, 1991.

British Standard Guide to the Principles of the Conservation of Historic Buildings, BS 7913, BSI,1998.

British Wood Preserving and Damp-Proofing Association (BWPDA), *The Installation of Remedial Damp Proof Courses in Masonry Walls: Code of Practice*, BWPDA, January 1997

Brunskill, R.W., *Brick Building in Britain*, Victor Gollancz, London, 1997.

Brunskill, R.W., *Illustrated Handbook of Vernacular Architecture*, Faber & Faber, London, 1999.

Brunskill, R.W., *Timber-Framed Buildings in Britain*, Victor Gollancz, London, 1999.

Brunskill, R.W., *Traditional Buildings of Britain*, Victor Gollancz, London.

Clifton-Taylor, A., *The Pattern of English Building*, Fourth Edition, Faber & Faber, London, 1987.

Collings, J., *Old House Care and Repair*, Donhead, Shaftesbury, 2002.

Cunnington, P., *Caring for Old Houses*, Second Edition, Marson House Publishers, Yeovil, 2002.

Curwell, S., Fox, B., Greenberg, M. and March, C., *Hazardous Building Materials: A guide to the selection of environmentally responsible alternatives*, Second Edition, Spon Press, London, 2002.

Davey, A., Heath, B., Hodges, D., Ketchin, M. and Milne, R., *The Care and Conservation of Georgian Houses*, Butterworth-Heinemann, Oxford, 1995.

Department for Transport, Local Government and the Regions, *The Building Regulations 2000, Approved Document L1: Conservation of fuel and power in dwellings* and *Approved Document L2: Conservation of fuel and power in buildings other than dwellings*, 2002 editions, The Stationery Office, 2002.

Department of the Environment/Department of National Heritage, *Planning Policy Guidance Note 15, Planning and the Historic Environment*, HMSO, London, 1994 (at the time of writing PPG15 is under review).

Dimes, F.G. and Ashurst, J., *Conservation of Building and Decorative Stone*, Butterworth-Heinemann, Oxford, 1998.

Earl, J., *Building Conservation Philosophy*, Third Edition, Donhead, Shaftesbury, 2003.

English Heritage, *Building Regulations and Historic Buildings: Balancing the needs for energy conservation with those of building conservation; an interim guidance note on the application of Part L*, English Heritage, September 2002.

English Heritage, *Framing Opinions:*
1 Draught Proofing, 2 Door and Window furniture, 3 Metal Windows, 4 Timber Sash Windows, 5 Window Comparisons, 7 Energy Savings

English Heritage, *Thatch and Thatching: a guidance note*, English Heritage.

Feilden, B., *Conservation of Historic Buildings*, Butterworth-Heinemann, Oxford, 2001.

The Georgian Group publishes advisory leaflets on the following subjects:
1 Windows; 2 Brickwork; 3 Doors; 4 Paint Colour; 5 Render Stucco and Plaster; 6 Wallpaper; 7 Mouldings; 8 Ironwork; 9 Fireplaces; 10 Roofs; 11 Floors; 12 Stonework; 13 Lighting; 14 Curtains and Blinds 15 Papier-mâché.

Harris, R., *Timber-Framed Buildings*, Shire Publications, Princes Risborough, 1993.

Historic Scotland, *Conservation and Repair of Sash Windows Practitioners Guide*, Historic Scotland, Edinburgh, 2002.

Historic Scotland, *External Lime Coating on Traditional Buildings*, Technical Advice Note 15, Historic Scotland, Edinburgh 2001.

Historic Scotland, *Performance Standards for Timber Sash and Case Windows*, Technical Advice Note 3, Historic Scotland, Edinburgh 1994.

Historic Scotland, *The Historical and Technical Development of the Sash and Case Window in Scotland*, Research Report, Historic Scotland, Edinburgh, 2001.

Hollis, M., *Surveying Buildings*, Fourth Edition, RICS Books, London, 2000.

Holmes, S. and Wingate, M., *Building with Lime: A practical introduction*, Intermediate Technology Publications, London, 1997.

Innocent, C.F., *The Development of English Building Construction* (1916 edition), Donhead, Shaftesbury, 1999.

Larsen, K., and Marstein, N., *Conservation of Historic Timber Structures – An ecological approach*, Butterworth-Heinemann, Oxford, 2000.

Lott, G.K., *Building Stone Resources of the United Kingdom*, 1:1,000,000 map, British Geological Survey, 2001.

London Hazards Centre, *Toxic Treatments: Wood preservative hazards at work and in the home*, London Hazards Centre Trust Limited, London, 1989.

Lynch, Gerard, *Brickwork, History, Technology and Practice*, Donhead, Shaftesbury, 1990.

Melville, I.A., and Gordon, I.A., *The Repair and Maintenance of Houses*, The Estates Gazette, London, 1997.

Minke, G., *Earth Construction Handbook: The building material earth in modern architecture*, WIT Press, Southampton, 2000.

Mynors, C., *Listed Buildings, Conservation Areas and Monuments*, Sweet & Maxwell, London, 1999.

Mynors, Charles, *The Law of Trees, Forests and Hedgerows*, Sweet & Maxwell, London, 2002.

Oliver, A., *Dampness in Buildings*, Second Edition, revised by Douglas, J. and Stirling, J.S., Blackwell Science, Oxford, 1997.

Pearson, Gordon T., *Conservation of Clay & Chalk Buildings*, Donhead, Shaftesbury, 1992.

Powys, A.R., *Repair of Ancient Buildings*, Third Edition, Society for the Protection of Ancient Buildings, London, 1995.

Ridout, B. (ed.), *English Heritage Research Transactions, Volume 4, Timber*, James and James Science Publishers, 2001.

Ridout, B., *Timber Decay in Buildings*, Spon Press, London, 2000.

Robson, P., *Structural Repair of Traditional Buildings*, Donhead, Shaftesbury, 1999.

Schofield, Jane, *Lime in Building: A practical guide*, Black Dog Press, Crendon, 1995.

Singh, J., *Building Mycology – Management of Decay and Health in Buildings*, E & FN Spon, London, 1994.

The Society for the Protection of Ancient Buildings (SPAB) Technical pamphlets and information sheets:

An Introduction to Building Limes, Information sheet 9.

Basic Limewash, Information sheet 1.

Care and Repair of Flint Walls, Technical pamphlet 16.

Care and Repair of Old Floors, Technical pamphlet 15.

Electrical Installations in Old Buildings, Technical pamphlet 9.

Introduction to Repair of Lime-ash and Plaster Floors, Information sheet 12.

Is Timber Treatment Always Necessary? An introduction for homeowners, Information sheet 14.

Patching Old Floorboards, Information sheet 10.

Removing Paint from Old Buildings, Information sheet 5.

Repair of Wood Windows, Technical pamphlet 13.

Re-pointing Stone and Brick Walling, Technical pamphlet 5.

Rough-cast for Historic Buildings, Information sheet 11.

Strengthening Timber Floors, Technical pamphlet 2.

The Care and Repair of Thatched Roofs, Technical pamphlet 10.

The Control of Damp in Old Buildings, Technical pamphlet 8.

The Need for Old Buildings to 'Breathe', Information sheet 4.

The Repair of Timber Frames and Roofs, Technical pamphlet 12.

The Victorian Society publish advisory leaflets on the following subjects:
1 Doors, 2 Decorative Tiles, 3 Fireplaces, 4 Interior Mouldings, 5 Wallcoverings, 6 Cast iron, 7 brickwork, 8 Paintwork, 9 Timber Windows.

Watt, D. and Swallow, P., *Surveying Historic Buildings*, Donhead, Shaftesbury, 1996.

Wood, M., *The English Mediaeval House*, Ferndale Editions, London, 1981.

Woolley, T., and Kimmins, S., *Green Building Handbook, Volume 2: A guide to building products and their impact on the environment*, Spon Press, London, 2002.

Woolley, T., Kimmins, S., Harrison, P. and Harrison, R., *Green Building Handbook, Volume 1: A guide to building products and their impact on the environment*, Spon Press, London, 2001.

Wright, A., *Craft Techniques for Traditional Buildings*, B.T. Batsford, 1991.

INDEX